To Milbu

an _old_ friend! :-

my best

Heucheras and Heucherellas

Heucheras and Heucherellas

Coral Bells and Foamy Bells

Dan Heims and
Grahame Ware

TIMBER PRESS
Portland · Cambridge

Published in 2005 by
Timber Press, Inc.
The Haseltine Building
133 S.W. Second Avenue, Suite 450
Portland, Oregon 97204-3527, U.S.A.

Timber Press
2 Station Road
Swavesey
Cambridge CB4 5QJ, U.K.

www.timberpress.com

Printed in Hong Kong

Library of Congress Cataloging-in-Publication Data

Heims, Dan.
    Heucheras and Heucherellas : coral bells and foamy bells / Dan Heims and Grahame Ware.
        p. cm.
      Includes index.
      ISBN 0-88192-702-3 (hardcover)
    1. Heuchera. 2. Heucherella. I. Ware, Grahame. II. Title.
      SB413.H52H45 2005
      635.9'3372—dc22
                                                                        2004015598
A Catalogue record for this book is also available from the British Library.

Contents

Color Plates

PLATE 1. *Heuchera* 'Amber Waves'.

PLATE 2. *Heuchera* 'Amber Waves' in the landscape.

Plate 3. *Heuchera americana* in the wild.

Plate 4. *Heuchera americana*, ruffled-leaf form.

Plate 5. *Heuchera americana* 'Eco-magnififolia'.

PLATE 6. *Heuchera americana* var. *hispida*, variegated.

PLATE 7. *Heuchera* 'Amethyst Myst'.

PLATE 8. *Heuchera* 'Appleblossom'.

Plate 9. *Heuchera* 'Autumn Haze'.

Plate 10. *Heuchera* 'Beauty Colour'. Photo by Chris Hansen.

Plate 11. *Heuchera* 'Black Beauty'.

Plate 12. *Heuchera* 'Can Can'.

Plate 13. *Heuchera* 'Canyon Pink'.

Plate 14. *Heuchera* 'Cappuccino'.

Plate 16. *Heuchera* 'Cascade Dawn'.

Plate 15. *Heuchera* 'Carousel'.
Photo by Chris Hansen.

PLATE 17. *Heuchera* 'Cathedral Windows'.

PLATE 18. *Heuchera* 'Champagne
Bubbles'. Photo by Mary Walters.

Plate 19. *Heuchera* 'Cherries Jubilee'.

Plate 20. *Heuchera* 'Chinook'.

Plate 23. *Heuchera* 'Chocolate Ruffles' with hoarfrost.

Plate 21. *Heuchera* 'Chiqui'.

Plate 22. *Heuchera* 'Chocolate Ruffles'.

Plate 24. *Heuchera* 'Chocolate Veil'.

Plate 26. *Heuchera* 'Crème Brûlée'. Photo by Chris Hansen.

Plate 25. *Heuchera* 'City Lights'.

PLATE 27. *Heuchera cylindrica*.

PLATE 28. *Heuchera* 'David'.

20

PLATE 29. *Heuchera* 'Ebony and Ivory'. Photo by Mary Walters.

PLATE 31. *Heuchera* 'Fireworks'.

PLATE 30. *Heuchera* 'Fandango'.

Plate 32. *Heuchera* 'Florist's Choice'.

Plate 34. *Heuchera* 'Geisha's Fan'.

Plate 33. *Heuchera* 'French Velvet'.

Plate 35. *Heuchera* 'Green Spice'.

Plate 36. *Heuchera* 'Gypsy Dancer'.

Plate 38. *Heuchera hirsutissima* 'Santa Rosa'.

Plate 37. *Heuchera hallii*.

Plate 39. *Heuchera* 'Hollywood'.

Plate 40. *Heuchera* 'Key Lime Pie'.

Plate 41. *Heuchera* 'Licorice'.

Plate 42. *Heuchera* 'Lime Rickey'.

PLATE 43. *Heuchera* 'Magic Wand'.

PLATE 44. *Heuchera* 'Mardi Gras'.

PLATE 45. *Heuchera* 'Marmalade'.

PLATE 46. *Heuchera micrantha* 'Martha Roderick'.

PLATE 47. *Heuchera micrantha* 'Ruffles'.

PLATE 48. *Heuchera* 'Mint Frost'.

PLATE 49. *Heuchera* 'Molly Bush'. Photo by Chris Hansen.

Plate 50. *Heuchera* 'Monet'.

Plate 51. *Heuchera* 'Obsidian'.

PLATE 52. *Heuchera parvifolia.*

PLATE 53. *Heuchera* 'Peach Flambé'.

PLATE 54. *Heuchera* 'Peach Melba'.

PLATE 56. *Heuchera* 'Peacock Feathers'.

PLATE 55. *Heuchera* 'Peachy Keen'. Photo by Mary Walters.

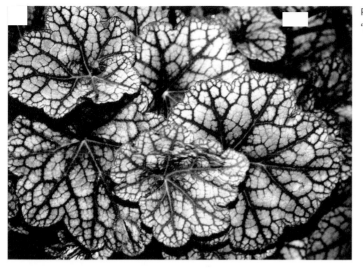

PLATE 57. *Heuchera* 'Persian Carpet'.

PLATE 58. *Heuchera* 'Petite Pearl Fairy'. Photo by Mary Walters.

PLATE 59. *Heuchera* 'Pewter Moon'.

Plate 60. *Heuchera* 'Pewter Veil'.

Plate 61. *Heuchera* 'Plum Pudding'.

Plate 62. *Heuchera pulchella*.

Plate 63. *Heuchera* 'Purple Mountain Majesty'.

Plate 64. *Heuchera* 'Purple Petticoats'.

PLATE 65. *Heuchera* 'Purple Sails'.

PLATE 66. *Heuchera*
'Rachel'—and Rachel.

PLATE 67. *Heuchera* 'Regal Robe'.

PLATE 68. *Heuchera* 'Ring of Fire'.

Plate 69. *Heuchera rubescens* var. *alpicola*.

Plate 70. *Heuchera* 'Ruby Veil'.

Plate 71. *Heuchera sanguinea*, Mexican form.

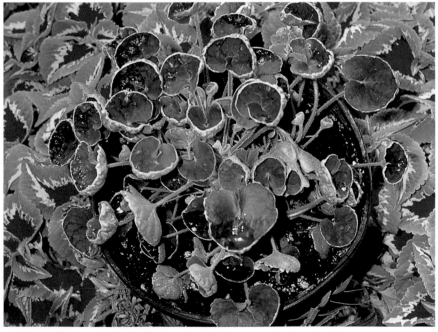

Plate 72. *Heuchera sanguinea* 'Fairy Cups'.

PLATE 73. *Heuchera sanguinea* 'Frosty'.

PLATE 74. *Heuchera sanguinea*
'Gold Dust'.

PLATE 75. *Heuchera sanguinea* 'Hailstorm'.

Plate 76. *Heuchera sanguinea* 'Snow Storm'.

Plate 77. *Heuchera sanguinea* 'Spangles'.

Plate 78. *Heuchera* 'Sashay'.

Plate 79. *Heuchera* 'Shamrock'.

PLATE 80. *Heuchera* 'Silver Indiana'.

PLATE 81. *Heuchera* 'Silver Scrolls'. Photo by Chris Hansen.

PLATE 82. *Heuchera* 'Silver Shadows'.

Plate 83. *Heuchera* 'Smokey Rose'.

Plate 84. *Heuchera* 'Snow Angel'.

PLATE 85. *Heuchera* 'Sparkling Burgundy'.

PLATE 86. *Heuchera* 'Sterling Silver'. Photo by Chris Hansen.

Plate 87. *Heuchera* 'Stormy Seas'.

Plate 88. *Heuchera* 'Strawberry Candy'.

Plate 89. *Heuchera* 'Strawberry Swirl'.

PLATE 90. *Heuchera* 'Tango'.

PLATE 91. *Heuchera* 'Velvet Night'.

PLATE 92. *Heuchera* 'Vesuvius'.

Plate 93. *Heuchera villosa* var. *macrorhiza*.

Plate 95. *Heuchera villosa* f. *purpurea*. Photo by Chris Hansen.

Plate 94. *Heuchera villosa* 'Melkweg'.

Plate 97. *Heuchera* 'White Spires'.

Plate 96. *Heuchera* 'Wendy'.

PLATE 98. *Heuchera* 'Winter Red'.

PLATE 99. *Heuchera* 'Zabeliana'.

PLATE 100. ×*Heucherella* 'Birthday Cake'.

Plate 101. ×*Heucherella* 'Bridget Bloom'.

Plate 102. ×*Heucherella* 'Burnished Bronze'.

Plate 103. ×*Heucherella* 'Checkered White'.

Plate 104. ×*Heucherella* 'Chocolate Lace'.

PLATE 105. ×*Heucherella* 'Dayglow Pink'. Photo by Mary Walters.

PLATE 106. ×*Heucherella* 'Kimono'.

Plate 107. ×*Heucherella* 'Party Time'.

Plate 108. ×*Heucherella* 'Rosalie'.

Plate 109. ×*Heucherella* 'Silver Streak'.

Plate 110. ×*Heucherella* 'Stoplight'.

Plate 111. ×*Heucherella* 'Sunspot'. Photo by Chris Hansen.

PLATE 112. ×*Heucherella* 'Viking Ship'.

PLATE 113. Crested mutant heuchera.

PLATE 115. Wand-type heucheras.

Plate 114. Variegated mutant heuchera.

PLATE 116. Heucheras in Ken Brown's garden.

CHAPTER 1

Heuchera in the Wild

The woodlands of North America abound in species of *Heuchera* and *Tiarella* and other members of the saxifrage family (Saxifragaceae). Most of these plants are little noticed by the casual observer: their flowers are small and mostly white or greenish, and their low-growing, softly textured foliage blends with its surroundings on the forest floor. The story of how these plants were found by Europeans, classified, brought into cultivation, and eventually made important elements in twenty-first-century gardens is a particularly good one, with a wow finish—an example of the way ornamental horticulture progresses over the centuries.

Discovery and description

The word "heuchera" was first used to describe the plant in 1738, with the publication of *Hortus Cliffortianus* by Carolus Linnaeus, the founder of binomial nomenclature, which system identifies organisms by genus and species (the first and second parts of their scientific names). *Heuchera americana*, found in eastern North America, is illustrated on page 82 of this sumptuous book, which was given away to friends by Linnaeus's patron, George Clifford, a wealthy English director of the Dutch East India Company; *Hortus Cliffortianus* depicts all the plants then grown on Clifford's estate, De Hartekamp, in Haarlem, The Netherlands.

Linnaeus named the genus *Heuchera* for Johann Heinrich von Heucher (1677–1747), a professor of medicine and botany at Wittenberg University in Germany and one of his friends and patrons, as well as the author of *Index Plantarum Horti Medici* (Index of plants in a physician's garden; 1711). For those who wish to use "proper" pronunciation, the genus is pronounced HOY-ker-uh, after Heucher. We have heard every permutation from who-CHAIR-uh to HEW-share-uh, but the proper way to pronounce a plant is to sound it as their namesake did—so, long-I CLIVE-ee-uh, *Clivia*, after Clive; FOR-scythe-ee-uh, *Forsythia*, after Forsythe; and so forth.

The heucheras in Clifford's garden are widely believed to have gotten there via John Clayton of Gloucester County, Virginia, but they undoubtedly came from specimens in the Leiden Botanic Garden, where we know the genus was being grown some forty years earlier, since it is shown under the name *Cortusa americana* in Paul Hermann's *Paradisus Batavus* (1698), the first comprehensive catalog of the plant material at Leiden. The original herbarium sheets received from Clayton (nos. 301 and 424) by Gronovius in 1735, which held the dried specimens on which Linnaeus may have based his description of provenance, were lost—perhaps before the Clifford Herbarium was established at the Natural History Museum of the British Museum, London, according to Charlie Jarvis of its staff; the specimen of *H. americana* now housed at the Natural History Museum was designated the lectotype (offi-

The "floribus" and "herbidis" of "Cortusa Americana" as illustrated in Paul Hermann's *Paradisus Batavus* (1698), page 130, plate 34.

cial representative of the species on file) in 1993 by James Reveal, Charlie Jarvis, and colleagues in "A List of Linnaean Generic Names and Their Types" (*Regnum Vegetabile* 127:54).

The power of the visual held sway for most of the seventeenth century. Clusius's *Rariorum Plantarum Historia* (1601) clearly shows the nomenclatural origins of *Heuchera*; as one can see in this book, there is an unmistakeable similarity between the woodcuts of "Sanicula Montana" (no. 246) and "Cortusa Mathioli" (no. 218), and influenced by these images, others came early on to refer to *Heuchera* as *Sanicula* and *Cortusa*.

Many sources list 1656 as the date of introduction of *Heuchera* to horticulture by the English nurseryman John Tradescant (the Younger), who is known from his catalog to have been growing it then, but illustrations of cultivated *H. americana* had appeared earlier in France. Robert Morison, named the first professor of botany at Oxford in 1669 and a friend of Hermann, had mentioned it in his *Hortus Regius Blesensis* (The royal garden at Blois; 1653 and 1655), as "Sanicula montana seu ['or'] Cortusa Americana." This work was cited in *Horto Joncquet* (1659) by Dionysius Joncquet, director of the Paris Jardin du Roi, who mentions "Sanicula montana peregrina seu Cortusa Americana" ("exotic mountain Sanicula or Cortusa Americana"), with authorship credit to Abel Brunyer (the gardener at Blois and author of record for the 1653 edition of *Hortus Regius Blesensis*), and "Sanicula Montana seu Cortusa Americana spicato herbaceo flore Robini," with credit to Vespasien Robin. It was Robin who may have published the very first reference, in his *Horto Regia Paris & Mentzel. Pugillo* (1623)—a catalog of "exotic plants from Québec, New England and Virginia"—as "Sanicula seu Cortusa Americana altera floribus minutus fimbriatus" ("Sanicula or Cortusa Americana, tiny and fringed with respect to the flowers"), and Joncquet's heuchera must have been growing in the Jardin du Roi before 1659.

Another, direct introduction of *Heuchera americana* to England was by the Reverend Banister, a pupil of Morison's at Oxford, who went to Virginia in 1678 and sent back collections and drawings that found their way into Morison's work as well as John Ray's *Historia Plantarum* (1704), which mentions "Cortusa Americana flore spicato" and cites Hermann's *Horto Lugd. Batavus* (1687). Joseph Pitton de Tournefort's *Institutiones Rei Herbariae* (1700, page 242) refers to "Mitella Americana florum petalis fimbriatus," perhaps the first instance of the word "mitella" (still a valid genus in the saxifrage family, with many American members) being applied to a heuchera.

In the modern classification, *Sanicula* is a genus in the Apiaceae (parsley family), and *Cortusa* is in the Primulaceae (primrose family). So similar are the leaves of *Cortusa* to those of *Heuchera*, however, that plant explorer André Michaux (1746–1802) named a subspecies of *H. americana* he found in the Carolina mountains *H. cortusa*. Michaux collected and named *H. villosa* as well as recollecting *H. americana* in the Carolinas and described them in his *Flora Boreali-Americana* (1803), the first truly scientific flora dealing entirely with American plants. Michaux's son, François, continued the work of his father and published a beautiful edition in three volumes (1810–13), followed by an exquisite English-language version published in Philadelphia under the title *North American Sylva* (1817–19).

The first nurseryman known to have offered *Heuchera americana* seed (in 1804) is Bernard M'Mahon (1775–1816) of Philadelphia, who produced the first seed catalog in the United States. M'Mahon, who championed the use of American native plants, also wrote *The American Gardener's Calendar* (1802), which became Thomas Jefferson's horticultural bible at Monticello.

Further botanizing of eastern North America would eventually disclose more species of *Heuchera*, but those species found west of the Great Plains are far more numerous and varied than those of the Atlantic coast. European botanists began to document these western species in the late eighteenth century, when Thaddeus Haenke and José Mariano Mociño collected *Heuchera* species along the coast of the Pacific Northwest during the expeditions of Malaspina and Quadra, respectively. Mociño's description of his 1792 collection, however, did not appear until after that by David Douglas, who published *H. micrantha* in 1826 and is therefore recognized as the authority for that species. A copy of a painting of the earlier Spanish collection by artist Atanasio Echeverría (a member of the Mociño expedition) was published in 1830 in de Candolle's *Prodromus* as plate 423, under the name *H. longipetala* (the original painting now resides in the Torner Collection at the Hunt Institute in Pittsburgh, Pennsylvania); it was not until 1936 that Rosedahl and colleagues determined that *H. longipetala* was a synonym for *H. micrantha* var. *diversifolia*. Seringe (*Prodromus* 4:52, 1830) also reported a specimen from Nootka Sound as *H. glabra*.

In August 1791, Haenke, botanist with the Malaspina expedition, visited the northwest coast of what we know as Vancouver Island in British Columbia. He collected what would later be named *Heuchera barbarossa*, published posthumously by the Czech botanist Karl Presl in *Relinquiae Haenkeanae* (1825–35), mere months behind Douglas's description of his collection of *H. micrantha* var. *diversifolia* from the Columbia River near The Dalles, Oregon.

Overland trips by hardy botanist-explorers to Mexico in the nineteenth century yielded *Heuchera sanguinea*, the species with the showiest flowers, and other trips brought *H. hallii*, *H. pulchella*, and *H. rubescens* from the mountains of New Mexico, Colorado, and California. Frederick Pursh (1774–1820), a Saxon immigrant, gained access—by means that have earned him some infamy among historians—to the collections and notes of the Lewis and Clark expedition, from which he cobbled together, under his own name, *Flora Americae Septentrionalis*, published in 1814 in London and Strasbourg. The first North American flora to include plants from the Pacific coast, it describes five species of *Heuchera*, three of which are still recognized: *H. pubescens* (which Pursh called *H. major*), *H. villosa* var. *villosa* (Pursh's *H. caulescens*), and *H. americana* var. *hispida* (Pursh's *H. scabra*).

Later came Yorkshireman Thomas Nuttall (1786–1859), who in 1808 in Philadelphia met Pursh and Benjamin Barton, an important patron of early American botany. Barton offered Nuttall eight dollars a month plus expenses to collect plants in the Northwest. Nuttall's explorations, interrupted by the War of 1812, came to fruition in the two slim volumes of *The Genera of North American Plants* (Philadelphia, 1818), which includes two *Heuchera* species authored by Nuttall: *H. parvifolia* and *H. ovalifolia* (now *H. cylindrica*). Nuttall would later collect in Ohio, Oklahoma, and the Arkansas Territory, but not until 1834 would he make it all the way to the Pacific coast.

David Douglas (1799–1834) discovered many plants of horticultural significance while in the employ of the Hudson's Bay Company. Not far from Fort Vancouver in present-day Washington State, sometime between 1825 and 1827, he found *Heuchera micrantha* and *H. cylindrica* along the Columbia River at a place he referred to as "Great Falls," presently The Dalles, Oregon. Two other giants of American botany, John Torrey (1796–1873) and Asa Gray (1810–1888), listed fifteen species of *Heuchera* in their *Flora of North America* (1838–43).

Ethnobotany

Before scientists ever examined and classified any plant, people were noting and using plants in medicine and cooking. The genus *Heuchera* is no exception. By far the most common American English name for *Heuchera* is alumroot, referencing its taste and indicating the strong medicinal qualities of the plant. Most often mentioned in older medical literature is *H. americana*, the source of the pharmaceutical heuchera, an astringent and antiseptic listed in formularies well into the twentieth century; analysis has shown that tannin is present in this species as well (Peacock and Peacock, *J. Am. Pharm. Assoc.* 16:729–737, 1927).

Medicinal Plants of North America (Merck 1912) reports that *Heuchera americana* was used by eastern Native Americans to treat sores, wounds, and ulcers, and as a base in powders meant to treat cancer; in Montana a combination of alumroots including *H. parvifolia* and *H. cylindrica* was used by natives as a remedy for diarrhea brought on by drinking water from alkaline lakes and streams.

Nancy Turner and her colleagues, in the excellent book *Thompson Ethnobotany* (1990), reports that native people of British Columbia used *Heuchera cylindrica* to cure gum boils: "The root is cut from the rest of the plant and cleaned and peeled. Once cleaned the root (about the size of a pea) is then put in the mouth. You chew it as you would chew tobacco. Do not swallow the juice." In the same book, a Thompson Salish woman relates that her grandmother used the mashed roots of *H. cylindrica*, covered with a cloth, as a poultice for boils or sores that would not heal—"and when she takes it off, the whole thing just kind of lifts up and sucks all the poison right out of the open cut." A tonic of the boiled roots was also found to be very useful for debility and fever, but roots intended for this treatment are best dug up before the plant flowers.

The *King's American Dispensatory* (1898) by Harvey Wickes Felter and John Uri Lloyd (http://www.ibiblio.org/herbmed/eclectic/kings/heuchera) offers an excellent and extensive history of the use of *Heuchera* from a pharmacological perspective.

CHAPTER 2

A Gardener's Guide to the Species

The genus *Heuchera* is a wholly North American member of the saxifrage family (Saxifragaceae). In fact, it is the largest herbaceous genus in that family that is confined entirely to North America, including Mexico. According to *Hortus Third* (1976), plants of this genus are herbaceous perennials with a tuft of rounded or broad 5- to 9-lobed toothed leaves that are heart-shaped at the base, from which, "overtopping the foliage," spring several slender scapes (leafless stalks) with "small, greenish, white, red or purplish" flowers (cup-, urn-, or saucer-shaped) produced in narrow panicles or racemes.

Simply speaking, all *Heuchera* species form rosettes at their base and produce long stalks with delicate flowers that open sequentially, beginning with the end of the stem.

The gardener interested in using heucheras may choose from many species, most of which are distinguished only by the degree of hairiness on their stems or the structure of their flower parts. We will furnish a simple but useful guide, written in terms accessible to the nonbotanist.

Woodlanders and crevice dwellers

Heuchera species are of two general types: woodland species (usually confined to the forests of eastern North America) and mountain species of the western Cordilleran region, the center of their diversity. We will call the former "woodlanders" and the latter "crevice dwellers." There are many more crevice dwellers than woodlanders, but the showier species tend to be the woodlanders of the Northeast. The crevice dwellers are mostly small and grow in rocky places, where their rhizome is a specialized adaptation for survival.

As gardeners using *Heuchera* species, we need to make sure that we keep their origins in mind when choosing their garden sites. In a woodland garden, many of the woodlanders and their hybrid kin (such as the *H. americana* hybrids) will fit in nicely. Someone with a dry western garden, by contrast, would be advised to choose crevice dwellers and their hybrids, which can take the aridity of summer and the cold (and possibly wet) winter conditions, including heavy snow loads. Woodland gardens with their shade and humus soil provide the situations needed by the lush, summer-growing woodlanders, while rock gardens or troughs may be better suited for crevice dwellers.

Writers have often been dismissive of the garden merit of *Heuchera* species (Christopher Grey-Wilson, in *A Manual of Alpine and Rock Garden Plants*, 1989, skips the genus entirely), but that seems to be changing. In *Complete Garden Guide to the Native Perennials of California* (1990), Glenn Keator is adamant: "Of all the woodland saxifrages, this genus is the easiest to grow and the most satisfactory in flower." Jack Elliott, in *Alpines in the Open Garden* (1991), commends four *Heuchera* species as excellent plants for sun or shade and makes a good case for their versatility, especially in difficult landscapes, allowing that *Heuchera* "also contains several species small enough for the rock garden or the front of a shady mixed border." And *H. cylindrica* 'Greenfinch' and two species heucheras make an appearance in Roger Phillips and Martyn Rix's *Perfect Plants* (1996).

A brief look at the species

Heuchera abramsii (Abram's alumroot, San Gabriel alumroot).
Named after an early California botanist. This species, found in the San Bernardino Mountains near Los Angeles, has pinkish red flowers.

Heuchera alba (white-flowered alumroot, white alumroot).
Found in Virginia and West Virginia in the Allegheny Mountains, it is similar in form and substance to *H. pubescens* but displays a little more vigor.

Heuchera alpestris (San Bernardino alumroot).
Found exclusively in San Bernardino County in California in red fir forests at elevations of between 6,000 and 8,000 feet. Some authorities treat this as a variety of *H. parishii*, but Elizabeth Wells and Barbara Shipes retain it as a separate species in their forthcoming monograph. Has white flowers and forms a cushion with age. Needs protection from winter rains and adequate drainage.

Heuchera americana (American alumroot).
Quite likely the most popular *Heuchera* species in American gardens. This woodland species has a wide area of distribution in the northeast of North America, ranging from southern Ontario down to the mountains of Georgia and from Indiana to New York State. Loves to grow in rich, rocky woods with shade in the afternoon preferred. It likes average to dry conditions and thus is a good understory plant. Large-lobed leaves, usually segmented into fives and toothed coarsely. Can get quite wide across (up to 1 foot) and high (6 to 12 inches). Long flower stalks (up to 2 feet) carry uninteresting greenish to purplish flowers. Many forms and varieties (var. *hispida*, for example) have beautiful foliage that is especially becoming in the spring and winter. This foundation woodlander is parent to an amazing array of excellent garden hybrids. Plates 3, 4, and 6.

Heuchera bracteata (bracted alumroot).
This species, found in Colorado and southern Wyoming, derives its specific epithet from the leafy bracts found at the end of its long stalks. Small leaves, just 2 to 3 centimeters across, in a rosette. Greenish creamy white flowers just 2 to 3 millimeters across. A definite crevice dweller, this species can often be found growing between the cracks of boulders at high elevations.

Heuchera brevistaminea (Laguna Mountains alumroot).
Found in the Laguna Mountains of San Diego County, California, at 6,000 to 8,000 feet, growing between cracks of boulders or perched on rock faces. Short stamens, as the epithet suggests, and not particularly floriferous. Spring-flowering (like most crevice dwellers) reddish flowers and reddish purple bracts.

Heuchera caespitosa (tufted alumroot).
Similar to *H. abramsii, H. alpestris, H. brevistaminea, H. elegans, H. hirsutissima,* and *H. pulchella*: for the rock garden in a drier climate.

Heuchera caroliniana (Carolina alumroot).
This species is restricted to a narrow band in North and South Carolina, in rich wooded uplands or moist, rocky outcrops of the Piedmont. Very small flowers (1/8 inch across) vary in color from white through pink; stalks can be as tall as 1 foot. It is very similar in appearance and size to *H. pubescens*. Wells has suggested that *H. caroliniana* is a southern extension of *H. pubescens*, from

which it may have evolved after the Pleistocene. A good plant for the sunny to partly shaded native meadow gardens of the Piedmont.

Heuchera chlorantha (green-flowered alumroot, meadow alumroot).
Not a particularly attractive plant, even by *Heuchera* standards! Found on the Pacific coast from British Columbia, including the Queen Charlotte Islands, to northern California in wet meadow and riparian habitats. Those who count *H. cylindrica* 'Greenfinch' a hybrid, improbable as that is, sometimes claim this species as a parent. Whitish flowers poorly displayed with green calyx on long stalks to 20 inches. A wild-garden candidate only.

Heuchera ×*cuneata* (*H. cylindrica* × *H. rubescens*).
A natural hybrid found in southern Oregon. It can be seen in some alpine gardens on the Pacific coast.

Heuchera cylindrica (circular alumroot).
One of the toughest crevice dwellers, ranging from Alaska to northeastern California at elevations from below 3,300 to above 9,800 feet. Also found in the Cordilleran range. Creamy flowers on long stalks. It's a candidate for the wild garden or crevice rock garden. Variety *alpina* has been very useful in breeding, creating dwarf plants with large flowers; larger forms are the parents of the Wand series. Plate 27.

Heuchera duranii (hard alumroot).
Found on rocky hills and in subalpine bristlecone pine forests at very high elevations (9,000 to 11,700 feet) in California and Nevada. This tiny rock garden plant has small flowers with a gold tone, which yellow coloration it has yielded to the flowers of some hybrids; a pink form is also reported. Some sources refer this species to *H. parvifolia*.

Heuchera ×*easthamii* (*H. chlorantha* × *H. micrantha*).
A natural hybrid found in British Columbia, with no particular beauty to recommend it to the gardener.

Heuchera eastwoodiae (Senator Mine alumroot).
Discovered by botanist Alice Eastwood on moist slopes in the Prescott area of central Arizona in 1935. Known for its variegated leaves. It grows at 8,200 to 11,500 feet and may be a southern variant of *H. parvifolia*.

Heuchera elegans (Bridger Mountain alumroot).
Found in Los Angeles County and Ventura County in the San Bernardino Mountains between 4,900 and 8,200 feet. Very attractive, larger-than-average white-pink flowers like little harebells. We have found it not terribly difficult to grow and keep in the drier areas of North America, especially in a dry perennial bed or a crevice rock garden. It is similar in many respects to other species in its area.

Heuchera flabellifolia (shortstem alumroot).
A small alpine species found high in the mountains of Idaho, Montana, and Nevada and into Alberta, Canada, growing in granitic or limestone cliffs or in settled talus from 6,600 to 9,800 feet. Small kidney-shaped leaves only 1/2 to 2 inches wide form compact rosettes flat on the ground. Creamy flowers are carried on long stalks, varying from 6 to 16 inches.

Heuchera glabra (smooth alumroot).
This glossy-leaved species can be found in a wide latitudinal swath from Mt. Hood, Oregon, to Alaska and from sea level to timberline. It takes quite a bit of moisture, as one would expect considering its maritime Northwest origins, and is hardy in northeast North America as well. White flowers are nicely displayed on strong, smooth stalks from 12 to 20 inches. Not surprisingly, given its large range, several forms occur within the species. It presents wonderful red-purple winter color and venation in cold areas, which makes the new green growth of spring seem that much more exciting. Like many *Heuchera* species, it can be relied upon to grow where many plants will not; this affords the creative gardener an opportunity to position it in spots like a dry, rocky corner or at the foot of boulders or the edges of pavement.

Heuchera glomerulata (Chiricahua Mountain alumroot).
A distinctive alpine species found in the Chiricahua Mountains of Arizona. Leaves are purplish green underneath and variegated on top, and the large purple-white flowers are held together in a compact cluster (glomerate), thus the epithet. It ought to be included in a breeding program: the variegated leaves might well attract variegatophiles.

Heuchera grossulariifolia (gooseberry-leaf alumroot).
Tiny alpine species found primarily in shady cliffs and crevices in Montana and Idaho, with some disjunct populations in the Columbia Gorge, near The

Dalles, Oregon. Generally it has creamy yellowish flowers on wiry stems varying from 6 to 20 inches. It has been researched extensively and found to
hybridize freely with *H. cylindrica*, with some resulting individuals carrying
twice the normal chromosome count. For the alpine or native plant gardener.

Heuchera hallii (Hall's alumroot).

This dwarf mountain heuchera hails from the high Colorado peaks. Tiny scalloped leaves only $3/8$ inch across form a rosette that itself only reaches 1 inch
after a few years. Bears a profusion of tiny white to pink flowers on wiry 4- to
6-inch stems. This one is definitely a worthwhile specimen for the alpine gardener. Plate 37.

Heuchera hirsutissima (shaggy-hair alumroot).

Found in the San Jacinto Mountains of Riverside County, California, between
7,200 and 11,500 feet. Beautiful selections with dark pink flowers have been
introduced. One of the showiest miniatures.

Heuchera longiflora (long-flower alumroot).

At first it is difficult to see the differences between this and *H. americana*; however, the horizontal orientation of the pink flowers, the tubular calyx, and the
fact that the petals cover the mouth of the flower easily distinguish this species. It is also the only species in the Northeast that is restricted to shaded
limestone outcroppings and substrates in Kentucky, Virginia, West Virginia,
Ohio, Alabama, and Tennessee.

Heuchera maxima (island alumroot).

This seaside dweller, a native of islands off the coast of California and in a few
disjunct places along the coast, is an exception to the western crevice dweller
association. A big-leaved plant (up to 7 inches) with long stalks (up to 20
inches), it makes a great groundcover but is not as hardy as most heucheras.
Light green leaves and creamy white flowers. Once established in partial shade
in the coastal areas of California, it does nicely without any summer watering
and as such is a good companion planting under the dry shade of oaks (plants
swallow the leaf litter and do not require the irrigation that is dangerous to
oaks); when given supplemental water (especially collected rainwater), it is a
happy and impressive bloomer. Many good garden hybrids have been derived
from this species, but these too are not as hardy as many other heucheras.

Heuchera merriamii (Merriam's alumroot).
Found in the Klamath Ranges of northern California and southern Oregon, growing in dry, rocky areas from 6,000 to 8,000 feet. A good candidate for the drier woodland garden, it doesn't require a crevice to be happy as long as its site is well drained. Grows up to 6 inches across and has lovely white flowers on 6- to 10-inch brown stalks. Leaves are usually a brighter shade of green, compared to the leaves of most heucheras. Neither too big nor too small for the open garden. It does well in western gardens and also in northeastern North America.

Heuchera micrantha (small-flowered alumroot).
This species likes more moisture than most western species and grows below 8,000 feet across a wide range of coastal western North America. Insignificant small white flowers over shallow-lobed green leaves. A few forms and varieties are worth keeping an eye out for, such as var. *diversifolia* from Vancouver Island, British Columbia, and the newly named var. *macropetala* from southern Oregon and northern California, which is the only stoloniferous heuchera known. The very hairy stems bear a striking similarity to *H. villosa*. This is the species that has lent "ruffles" to many of our garden hybrids.

Heuchera novomexicana (New Mexico alumroot).
Found in Arizona in Coconino County, growing at elevations between 8,000 and 12,000 feet. Disjunct populations are also found in southwestern New Mexico and in the San Pecos range in northwest Texas. Not particularly garden-worthy.

Heuchera parishii (Parish's alumroot, Mill Creek alumroot).
A denizen of the San Bernardino Mountains, growing between 6,000 and 11,200 feet. Wants extreme drainage. It was thought to have been a natural hybrid between *H. rubescens* and *H. hirsutissima* until chemotaxonomy testing ruled that out. Flowers are similar to *H. hirsutissima* but fewer and on short spikes.

Heuchera parviflora (little-flower alumroot).
A species that ranges all over the southeast of North America including many Midwest states, growing on sandstone ledges in complete shade. This adaptation to an "ecological island" supports its survival. It is unique among heucheras for two reasons: it has smooth seeds (most heuchs have rough

seeds), and the new leaves are sticky—what botanists call viscid. Flowers are usually white, tipped with green.

Heuchera parvifolia (little-leaf alumroot).

Found at elevations of 6,000 to 14,000 feet from Arizona, New Mexico, Colorado, Utah, Wyoming, Nevada, and Idaho. Creamy yellow calyx and creamy white green-tipped flowers on short stems to 6 to 10 inches. It is strictly a wild-garden or collector's subject. Plate 52.

Heuchera pilosissima (seaside alumroot).

Found on the ocean bluffs and shady slopes of the north coast of California down to Santa Barbara. Stems 6 to 10 inches with pink-red flowers. A definite wild-garden candidate in the warmer parts of the West, but does not flourish in northeastern North America.

Heuchera pubescens (downy alumroot).

A handsome and tough customer that lives on the rock ledges and shale barrens of south-central Pennsylvania, Maryland, and West Virginia. A robust plant on the scale of *H. americana*, but everything on it is just a notch smaller and more refined. Rose-pink flowers (often with white tips) are held on strong stems covered with downy hairs, thus the name. An excellent cut flower as well. Its green leaves, usually mottled silver, are 3 to 4 inches wide and nicely lobed. Possibly the most sun-proof woodlander (at least in the North) and a good companion to lime-loving alpines as well as dwarf conifers. Charles Oliver used this species heavily in his breeding.

Heuchera pulchella (Sandia Mountains alumroot).

Similar to *H. hallii* but more diminutive, a New Mexico cousin from the Sandia Mountains. Also found in the Manzano and San Juan Mountains. It prefers limestone cliffs. Everything on this species is smaller, with the added allure of pinkish red flowers with a noticeable fringed margin. One collection that many alpine gardeners (ourselves included) have found attractive came from seed gathered at the 10,600-foot elevation in Bernalillo County, New Mexico, offered by Gwen Kelaidis through Rocky Mountain Rare Plants tagged as 92-255; this very floriferous seed strain is excellent in the trough and rock garden. Plate 62.

Heuchera richardsonii (Richardson's alumroot).
Wide range, growing on upland prairies and bluffs, in dry woods and sandy fields throughout the prairies of Canada, extending into northern Manitoba and across to northern Alberta to the southern Yukon and Northwest Territories. Overlaps with *H. americana* in Indiana. Coarse leaves, very much resembling a geranium, about 2 inches across. Flowers are variable but usually green-creamy and on stalks ranging in height from 12 to 24 inches. A useful plant for the wild or native garden in cooler continental climates, it is a parent (along with *H. sanguinea*) of the cold-hardy hybrids 'Ruby Mist', 'Brandon Glow', and 'Northern Fire', bone-hardy heucheras that are staples of the prairie perennial garden.

Heuchera rubescens (pink alumroot).
Found in dry, rocky places from 6,600 to 13,100 feet in the Sierra Nevada, California, and over to New Mexico and Arizona as far as the Trans Pecos Mountains in Texas and down into the Sierra Madre Occidental range in Mexico. A diverse species with many varieties. Bright green leaves form tight rosettes that can become beautiful wide mats under ideal circumstances in the wild. Foamy white flowers with pink bracts are displayed on short, strong stems from 6 to 12 inches. Variety *alpicola* is grown to perfection at the Denver Botanic Gardens. Many varieties have shocking pink flowers; this coloring depends to some degree on the minerals in the soil and the amount of nutrients available to the plant. It is a prime candidate for the alpine gardener to experiment with or for the lowland gardener who wants a very tough pot plant that flowers over a long period while standing up to benign neglect. Dara Emery used this species in his breeding. Plate 69.

Heuchera sanguinea (coral bells).
This is the plant that has given garden heucheras their common name, and "coral" is its distinguishing feature. The species ranges to some very high altitudes; Alan Bradshaw's recent Alplains Seeds catalog offers var. *pulchra*, which he collected at 6,800 feet in Cochise County, Arizona, growing in crevices of a north-facing granite cliff, and plantsman Sean Hogan has seen other sanguineas living in the shadows of cactus in the Chihuahuan Desert in Mexico. By using seed collections from extreme habitats, breeders can stretch the usual limits for heucheras.

Hummingbirds cannot resist this plant, and every garden should have it in lieu of garish plastic hummingbird feeders. For more than a century breeders, starting with Victor and Émile Lemoine, have used this plant to impart color. It makes an excellent cut flower as well. Many good seed strains exist, including *H. sanguinea* 'Leuchtkäfer. Plate 71.

Heuchera villosa (hairy alumroot).

A highly variable summer-flowering species that occurs over a wide range east of the Mississippi River. Variety *arkansana* occurs in the Arkansas Ozarks and var. *villosa* in the southern Appalachian Mountains—a mere two hundred miles separates them. Many forms of this species, including var. *macrorhiza*, are useful for southeastern North American gardens, in either woodland or mixed perennial plantings. They also adapt nicely to western North American gardens, where moist, rich woodland conditions exist or can be created. It is strictly a foliage plant, with insignificant flowers, but nursery people occasionally find a good form of a species and clone it. An example in this species' case is Charles Oliver's 'Bronze Wave', a selection of the purple form (f. *purpurea*) of var. *villosa*. Bears a strong resemblance to the western *H. micrantha*. Plates 93 and 95.

Heuchera wootonii (White Mountains alumroot).

The White Mountains in this case are those in Lincoln County, New Mexico. Also found in the Datil Mountains. This is a white-flowered species found usually on north-facing rock outcrops or in oak thickets in the montane zone between 6,600 and 11,500 feet. Further work by botanists might see this lumped into *H. parvifolia*.

Exclusively Mexican species

Many of the aforementioned species in the Southwest of the United States, including *Heuchera sanguinea* and *H. rubescens*, range south into Mexico; and perhaps *H. townsendii* and *H. mexicana* may be southern variants of those species. Here we will list only those species not included earlier. Carl Otto Rosendahl and his colleagues Frederic Butters and Olga Lakela did work on the Mexican species in the 1930s, and much of what we know is based on their monograph of *Heuchera*, published by the University of Minnesota Press in 1936. The four Mexican species that follow were grouped together as section *Rhodoheuchera* by Rosendahl et al., who declared of them, "Nowhere in the genus is there such a tangle of involved relationships and intergrading forms."

Heuchera acutifolia (sharp-leaved alumroot).
Collected near Trinidad, Hidalgo State, by Rose in 1904. Found at 6,600 feet
on moist ledges and banks, usually north-facing. This one has beautifully
pointed heart-shaped leaves of some substance and size (up to 2 inches), unlike most of the crevice dwellers of higher elevations, with their rather tight
scalloped leaves. Bristly brown hairs on the surface of the leaves. Nice white
flowers with pink sepals give a lovely contrast. Might prove to be a good ele-
ment of a hybridizing program.

Heuchera amoena (pleasant alumroot).
Collected near Monterrey, Nuevo León State, in 1906 at 2,600 feet along moist,
shaded banks. Small flowers on quite an open and sparse structure. Deeply
lobed leaves.

Heuchera hemsleyana (Hemsley's alumroot).
Collected by Hemsley in the mountains in three different states (Michoacán,
Morelos, and Puebla) in Mexico. Pink flowers on long stalks.

Heuchera orizabensis (Orizaba alumroot).
The most southerly of all *Heuchera* species. Collected by Hemsley in the Sierra
de San Felipe in Oaxaca and in Puebla State near the peak of Orizaba, from
which it derives its epithet. Like most other Mexican species, it has bristly
brown hairs on somewhat sticky leaves. Fairly large $1/4$-inch pink flowers on
stalks anywhere from 8 to 20 inches.

Family ties

Saxifragaceae, early in its evolutionary history, split into two clans (or clades),
with *Saxifraga* evolving along a largely arctic-alpine route and *Heuchera* being
primarily temperate and montane. Within *Heuchera*'s clan, the greatest bio-
diversity can be seen in western North America, where most other genera of
the North American Saxifragaceae (*Bensoniella, Bolandra, Darmera, Elmera, Lep-
tarrhena, Lithophragma, Suksdorfia, Tellima, Tolmiea*) are found as well.

    Heuchera, which arose and evolved in the western mountains and valleys,
is considered to be among the most advanced members of its clan and, indeed, the whole family. This view is based on its predominantly half-inferior
ovary and more or less zygomorphic (symmetrically bilateral) flowers. The

western species are more diverse than their eastern cousins; the high mountains and valleys throughout the Rocky Mountain Cordillera isolated more small populations than was the case in the more evenly glaciated east. The center of the glacial action in eastern North America occupies what is now Ungava Bay in northern Quebec, which explains the underrepresentation of *Heuchera* in the New England states.

What actually constitutes a species has been much discussed over the years. John Torrey and Asa Gray recognized just fifteen species when they did the first taxonomic treatment of *Heuchera* in 1841; they based their analysis on the structural features of the flowers and subdivided the genus into sections based on three morphological features: degree of exsertion of the stamens and styles beyond the calyx; pronounced bilateral symmetry of the flower, and the length of the flower from the ovary base to the sepal tips.

In 1890 Wheeler recognized twenty-one species and eight varieties, but his work was soon eclipsed: in 1905 Rydberg of the New York Botanical Garden published his North American Flora, in which the number of *Heuchera* species (including several collections from Mexico that modern floras of North America—BIOTA, for example—do not treat) exploded to seventy-two. Hard on the heels (a week after its publication) of Rydberg's count came that of Rosendahl, who pegged the number of *Heuchera* at twenty-seven. Rosendahl wasn't finished with this genus, however, as we have heard. Thirty-one years later, working with Butters and Lakela at the University of Minnesota, Rosendahl generated the first significant modern monograph on *Heuchera*, one that included investigations into the interfertility of the species as well. An incredible amount of personal fieldwork went into this very thorough treatment, which named 109 species and subspecies all told; the three colleagues traveled from Alaska, all over British Columbia and the Pacific Northwest and on down to Mexico, and gathered all the herbarium specimens they could, from everywhere, as well as the notes accompanying them. Their monograph was a watershed work and has provided the modern standard.

Elizabeth Wells, associate professor of botany at George Washington University, has done more work on this genus than anyone over the last twenty years. Along with her colleague Barbara Shipes of Hampton University in Virginia (who specializes in the western *Heuchera* species), she has come up with the best current classification of the genus, which we use in this book; their forthcoming monograph identifies thirty-six species and thirty-seven subspecies, as well as two natural hybrids. According to Wells (1984), *Heuchera* is typified by "variable diagnostic characters and intergrading species (merging into one another in a series of types). . . . The reliance on morphological characters in taxonomic treatments of *Heuchera* has led to a confusing array of specific and infraspecific names, applied to barely distinguishable taxa."

In her molecular biological work, Wells has employed flavonoid testing—but she has not abandoned morphological characteristics completely when attempting species identification. Among spring-blooming taxa of the eastern species, the most valuable characteristic for species recognition is the length of the free hypanthium, a ring- or tube-like structure formed by the enlargement and fusion of the basal portion of the calyx, corolla, and stamens, together with the receptacle (sometimes called the floral cup). Each of the eastern species is distinctive in this regard. Wells's work indicates a sectional affinity among *Heuchera americana, H. caroliniana, H. longiflora, H. pubescens,* and *H. richardsonii,* and again between *H. parviflora* and *H. villosa.* It should come as no surprise that natural hybridization and intergradations between the species were discovered. For the most part, however, temperature zones appear to be a restricting factor in intergrading, because temperature intolerance is a limiting factor. Within the aforementioned eastern species, the overlapping occurs mainly between *H. pubescens* and *H. americana* in the mountains of Virginia and West Virginia; and *H. americana* and *H. richardsonii* in Indiana.

Researchers Kari Segraves and John Thompson at Washington State University discovered autotetraploids (natural tetraploids—ones with two copies of a single haploid set) and triploids during their research on *Heuchera grossulariifolia* in Idaho (*Molecular Ecology* 8; 1999); the tetraploids tended to have larger flowers and attracted a more varied group of pollinators. The typical chromosome count for *Heuchera* is 2n = 14, but several autotetraploid species tested by Doug Soltis (results published in 2001) have been found to contain the count of 2n = 28. Soltis, who has been doing molecular research on *Heuchera* and the Saxifragaceae for decades, has recently integrated all his phylogenetic research with that of flavonoid and karyotypic data to suggest that a revision of the genus is in order.

Some experts argue, however, that with groups as interfertile as *Heuchera,* a strictly cladistic approach is unreasonable. They hold that even if basic, deep-level relationships are found, they have been subjected to so much recent polyploidy that it is difficult, if not impossible, to trace the gene flow.

CHAPTER 3

Breeding *Heuchera*

Breeding is a very involved process that requires discipline, order, *and* a good eye. A breeder must wear many hats—artist, botanist, horticulturist, geneticist, and judge and executioner. Let's examine these personas and see how they work and play themselves out within the breeding process.

The artist

Every artist is a dreamer who has a vision of what could be and an intrinsic need to buck the status quo. This visionary feels compelled to pull us out of the mundane abyss we call reality, stimulating us mentally and exciting us with a sense of fun. The artist is creative, naturally, and seeks creative ways to reach his or her goal. The artist, however, needs to call upon the botanist for help in this quest.

The botanist

Imagine an artist with only one color at his or her disposal. The botanist fills the artist's palette with the colors and textures of the species and the artist's mind with dreams of the combinations that could result. Each species adds its own attributes, and the botanist must make a list of available species and add their traits to the artist's mix. Here are some of the traits a botanist would consider worth a close look:

Heuchera americana—evergreen, leathery, dark green leaves, purplish winter color, vivid venation, insignificant flowers, silvering.
Heuchera cylindrica—strong flower stalks with large flowers, chartreuse flowers, some silvering on the leaves, tall flowers.

Heuchera hallii, H. merriamii, H. rubescens (montane forms)—tiny foliage, some variation in flower colors, dwarf habit.

Heuchera maxima—large foliage and clumps, tall flowers, hairiness, not terribly winter hardy.

Heuchera micrantha—small flowers of white or pink, hundreds of flowers on a stalk, ruffled foliage.

Heuchera pubescens—rose-pink flowers, strong stems, large taproot makes it a good summer-hardy species.

Heuchera richardsonii—small flowers of rusty red, many-flowered.

Heuchera sanguinea—xeric traits, best color spectrum from white to deepest red, tight mounds of foliage, good-sized flowers.

Heuchera villosa—tiny cream flowers, very large leaves, purple leaves in some varieties.

The botanist can source and acquire seed or plants. The next step is identifying pollination structures in the plant, at which point the botanist hands the borrowed artist's palette, now augmented with the above set of leads, to the horticulturist.

The horticulturist

The horticulturist receives the plants and raises them to flowering maturity. Another layer of expertise is added by the horticulturist: knowledge of a plant's blooming time and especially the quirks or weaknesses or strengths of the species used, as follows:

Heuchera americana—tough, shade-tolerant, no mildew problems, good variation in coloring, long petioles, tolerance of high heat and humidity combined.

Heuchera cylindrica—some mildew susceptibility.

Heuchera hallii, H. merriamii, H. rubescens (montane forms)—intolerance of high heat and humidity combined, extreme hardiness, early bloom.

Heuchera maxima—intolerance of high heat and humidity combined, less hardy than most.

Heuchera micrantha—intolerance of high heat and humidity combined, good mildew resistance.

Heuchera pubescens—sun-tolerant.

Heuchera richardsonii—extreme hardiness and scope, strong stalks.

Heuchera sanguinea—much mildew susceptibility, intolerance of high heat and humidity combined.

Heuchera villosa—tolerance of high heat and humidity combined, very late bloomer.

Only through extensive trials in multiple locations can the shortcomings be overcome by creative breeding. The plants that make the cut are primed for pollination and can be kept in a cooler to delay flowering (or pollen can be stored) for the geneticist.

The geneticist

Much time is saved by not attempting the impossible, and for starters, the geneticist must determine the chromosome counts of the plants he or she is working with. Some genera (*Chrysanthemum*, for instance) have species with chromosome counts ranging from fourteen to eighty. Do all *Heuchera* species have the same chromosome count? Most do: 2n = 14 (the natural tetraploids, as we learned in chapter 2, will have a chromosome count of 2n = 28); *Tiarella*, by the way, also has fourteen chromosomes and will cross (reluctantly) with *Heuchera*, yielding foamy bells, ×*Heucherella*.

With the genetic makeup known, the geneticist works with the artist, the botanist, and the horticulturist by setting the breeding aims, plotting the cross, and discovering a proper mechanism for pollination. The pollen can be applied to the pistil of the pod-parent by using plucked stamens or a pollen-coated pipe cleaner or brush; removing the stamens (emasculization) for this purpose is much more difficult in *Heuchera* than in *Hemerocallis* (daylily). Some species, *Heuchera americana* for one, are prodigious pollen producers and show some tendency for wind pollination. It is important to keep stray pollen and pollinating insects off of your project: using a screened greenhouse is a must. Timing is critical; stigmas are receptive (sticky) at different times.

Once the crosses are made, they are recorded on a small tab and tied to the pod—challenging work with a flower $^1/_{16}$ inch long! Further records are kept in a cross-book with the date of pollination. Crosses are frequently done on both parents reciprocally.

The ensuing seed and new plants (F_1, or first generation) are observed for dominant traits and any hint as to which of the recessive traits may show up in the F_2 (second) generation, which group of seedlings is the result of selfing (self-pollinating) the F_1 group. Well-labeled F_2 plants are given to the horticulturist to raise for evaluation by the judge and executioner.

Judge and executioner

Ruthlessness is a good trait in a breeder. The most exciting and tragic role a breeder must play is a dual one, that of judge and executioner, eliminating thousands of seedlings before they see the light of the sun as adults. At Terra Nova, plants are grown on in the greenhouse and in the field—over an acre of land in intense cultivation, just to keep these hybrids in the best of care. A three-year evaluation period follows, where professionals and novices alike judge plants. Two waves of judging usually occur, one for foliage and the other for flowers. In this democratic process, any plant receiving multiple flags for both foliage and flowers is given a breeding number, HE-01-127 (A33-7-8), for example, as follows:

Genus and trial year (HE-01)
Individual number (127)
Exact location in the field (A33-7-8): field A, bed 33, row 7, position 8

This way, any member of the Terra Nova staff for any reason can locate a single plant. The number is written on a large tag along with any unique features or special traits, like bloom time or number of flower stalks. By the end of the three-year period, a top selection simultaneously undergoes tissue-culture trials and is sent to multiple sites around the world for trials under different climactic conditions. Terra Nova produces some of the most high-priced composting material ever created. That's the downside. The upside is that with good feedback, a final selection is made, and, with the proper amount of rum and Coke, the plant receives a fitting name.

Plant patents are always applied for (abbreviated PPAF), as too many pirate labs in Holland, Canada, and the United States are very quick to steal a plant. As one can imagine, much money and time is spent to develop new varieties, and these "Jolly Roger" tissue-culture labs are continually firing broadsides just outside the final docking of a plant cultivar. They aim to down not only the Terra Nova ship but others as well. Once it is finally patented (at no small cost), the plant is then marketed worldwide.

To those of you who wish to do breeding (and we do encourage you to do so): please discard the second-rate plants. All too often, daylily breeders sell their less-than-perfect hybrids, adding to a miserable mess that a genus with a hundred thousand different varieties can't afford. Unless we wish a second chance with a plant, we put on our judge-and-executioner hat, throw them in the compost, and return them to the soil. Sloppy, open-pollinated breeding like the kind that is occurring in Holland is equally reprehensible and rarely results in a stellar plant. It severely dilutes the impact of the quality plants currently in the market that *have* been put through their paces as just outlined; and the damage is compounded, as these randomly wind- and bee-pollinated plants are typically not trialed in North America, which gives them no claim to garden merit. This leads to confusion for the nursery people as well as the home gardener. Again, if one looks at the situation with daylilies and hostas, we see historically how things can quickly go downhill.

CHAPTER 4

Heuchera Moves to the Garden: Hybrids and Hybridizers

Natural hybrids of *Heuchera* are not common, so it was left to gardeners to discover the heritable traits of the different species and to produce the garden-worthy hybrids we now enjoy.

Classic *Heuchera* breeders

Lemoine et Fils

Serious hybridizing began in the latter part of the nineteenth century with Victor Lemoine and his son Émile, whose nursery, Lemoine et Fils, was located at Nancy, France. Véronique Detriché of La Grange aux Vivaces nursery in Chanteloup, France, relates that Victor and Émile were "crazy" hybridizers, working on a vast number of genera; the Lemoines are perhaps best known for their work on hydrangeas, *Philadelphus* (mock oranges), and *Syringa* (lilacs), but Victor and especially Émile also worked with *Heuchera*. In 1897 they introduced 'Brizoides'—the basis for many great modern hybrids—and went on to produce a string of dazzling introductions, including 'Gracillima' (1900); 'Flambeau' and 'La Perle' (1901); 'Fantaisie', 'Grenade', and 'Pluie de Feu' (1902); 'Caprice' and 'Ondine' (1903); 'Rubis' and 'Virginal' (1904); 'Cascade', 'L'Africain', 'Lumière', and 'Sanglant' (1905); 'Albatros', 'Orphée', and 'Panorama' (1906); 'Fusée', 'Pléiade', and 'Saturnale' (1907); 'Clocheton', 'Cyclone', and 'Radium' (1908); and in 1920, after the hiatus of World War I, 'Argus', 'Eden', and 'Hermès'.

Victor Lemoine was the first non-English person to win the Veitch Memorial Medal from the Royal Horticultural Society; and 'Gracillima', the first hybrid heuchera to win an Award of Merit (AM) from the RHS, was the pod parent to many subsequent Lemoine cultivars, including 'Amourette' (1905), 'Girandole' (1904), 'Labyrinthe' (1905), 'Nébuleuse' (1906), 'Poésie' (1907), and 'Profusion' (1904). 'Ondine' was described as a superior variety of *Heu-*

chera alba (read, *H. sanguinea* 'Alba'). The first with bronze-marbled foliage was 'Fantaisie', followed by 'Cascade' and 'Labyrinthe'. 'Sanglant' was the first with silver marbling. 'Pluie de Feu' has had considerable staying power, both as a cultivar and as a seed parent. Many fine Lemoine cultivars are still available in France, but nowhere else.

Alan Bloom

There was little interest in heucheras in England at the end of the nineteenth century, a period of lavish gardens where subtle plants like coral bells tended to be disfavored by gardeners. In *Alan Bloom's Hardy Perennials* (1991), the author mentions that only two heucheras were purchased by his father, Charles Bloom, in Wisbech in 1919: *Heuchera sanguinea* 'Trevor Red' and the hybrid 'Gracillima'. Charles Bloom trialed the plants at their nursery in Oak-

Alan Bloom.

ington, Cambridgeshire, England, as potential cut flowers. Rows of these two varieties yielded open-pollinated seedlings that Alan, then in his teens, and his father evaluated. To their delight, several showed marked improvement ('Bloom's Variety' received an AM from the RHS in 1930). In 1931, the elder Bloom moved away, leaving Alan in Oakington, where he pursued his passion, procuring many French *Heuchera* cultivars. At the 1934 Chelsea Flower Show, Alan presented a display composed entirely of heucheras, including nine new cultivars, but sales were so disappointing that year that he did not put on another show for thirty-one years! Through the war years, Alan continued to raise thousands of heucheras and was able to test some of the best at the Trial Gardens of RHS Wisley. In 1946, Alan quit Oakington and bought Bressingham Hall, in Norfolk; by the 1950s, he had developed an excellent seed strain, the Bressingham Hybrids, as well as thirteen named clones. Blooms breeder Percy Piper worked with him on these seed strains and cultivars, many of which selections are still grown. *Heuchera* species involved in the Blooms of Bressingham breeding program include *H. americana*, *H. cylindrica*, *H. micrantha*, and *H. villosa*.

In 1998 Dan visited Alan Bloom, who—even at ninety-two years of age— had been out that very morning hybridizing heucheras. His passion for and dedication to the genus has truly earned him status as the "godfather of heucheras."

Lee W. Lenz

Lenz, an important botanist working with California native plants, completed his Ph.D. at the Missouri Botanical Garden under Edgar Anderson and started work at California's Rancho Santa Ana Botanic Garden, near Pomona, California, in 1948. In 1960 he was named director, a position he held until his retirement in 1983. His early research centered on cytogenetics and taxonomy, especially in the lily and iris families. He is also interested in the origin of cultivated plants and has carried out horticultural breeding programs at the RSABG, utilizing such native western plants as *Heuchera maxima* and *H. sanguinea*. Heucheraphiles know him best for large, floriferous hybrids such as 'Genevieve', 'Susanna', 'Wendy', and 'Santa Ana Cardinal', the results of crosses between the aforementioned species.

Dara Emery

Dara Emery was one of the contributing authors on *Heuchera* in the most recent (1993) edition of *The Jepson Manual: Higher Plants of California*. He

started working at the Santa Barbara Botanic Garden in 1955 as its first horticulturist and became its first full-time plant breeder in 1981. Emery championed the use of native plants in garden landscapes, and this bent carried over
into his teaching and breeding programs. 'Canyon Delight' and 'Canyon Pink',
two of his best heucheras, were developed after he decided that his criteria
were compact form, uniform leaves, and "flower power." At one time in the
early 1980s, he had thousands of crosses growing in the trial fields. After inten-
sive testing, fewer than a hundred from this group were selected for further trials. Emery retired in 1990 and died two years later, having made an invaluable
contribution to modern "California-style" hybrid heucheras. Other Dara
Emery hybrids, some of which were released by the Santa Barbara Botanic
Garden after their breeder's death, include 'Canyon Belle', 'Canyon Chimes',
'Canyon Duet', 'Canyon Melody', 'Blushing Bells', and 'Pink Wave'.

Henry Marshall and Lynn Collicutt

The Morden Research Station, near Brandon, Manitoba, is Canada's only gov-
ernment-funded research station specializing in ornamental plants. It is especially well known for its many cold-hardy rose introductions, but researchers
have also worked on heucheras, a project H. H. (Henry) Marshall initiated in
the early 1980s and Lynn Collicutt subsequently carried on. Marshall aimed
to create ornamentals that would tolerate the "prairie cold" of the northern
Great Plains, and indeed his hybrid heucheras proved tolerant of incredible
cold, even down to -40F. He introduced three hardy *Heuchera* cultivars there
in 1983, 'Brandon Glow', 'Brandon Pink', and 'Northern Fire'; 'Ruby Mist'
came later, a result of Collicutt's work. Other seedlings with flower colors of
white, cream, greenish, pink, chartreuse, red, and scarlet-red were also produced during these trials but not introduced. No one at Morden is currently
working with *Heuchera*.

Recent *Heuchera* breeders

Carol Bornstein

Dara Emery's work is now carried on by Carol Bornstein, a real expert on
natives and a promoter of heuchera use in the garden. She is a director at the
Santa Barbara Botanic Garden.

Allen Bush

A Southern gentleman, Allen Bush was instrumental in improving the lot of *Heuchera villosa* f. *purpurea* 'Palace Purple' with his superior glossy purple-leaved selection of it, 'Molly Bush', named for his daughter.

David Fross

David Fross of Native Sons Nursery in Arroyo Grande, California, seeks "to experiment with new selections with the intention of adding a sense of exploration and discovery to California gardens." His vision has brought a plethora of new heucheras to the U.S. Southwest scene.

Nancy Goodwin

Serendipity smiled upon Nancy Goodwin, whose sharp horticultural eyes discovered *Heuchera* hybrids of garden merit from open pollination, especially the seminal 'Montrose Ruby'. This hybrid between *H. americana* 'Dale's Strain' and *H. villosa* f. *purpurea* 'Palace Purple' combined for the first time the purple foliage color found in some wild individuals of the southeastern species *H. villosa* and its var. *macrorhiza* with the silvery leaf mottling of *H. americana*. Her Montrose Nursery is now closed, but her lovely gardens in Hillsborough, North Carolina, remain a delight to all who enter.

Dale Hendricks

Dale Hendricks, alias "the Lizard of Landenberg," runs North Creek Nurseries, a large wholesale perennial nursery, with business partner Steve Castorani. Dale is best known for *Heuchera americana* 'Dale's Strain', a variable group which has provided the nucleus for many metallic-leaved forms.

Don Jacobs

The breeding pool would not have been so richly deep had it not been for the efforts of Don Jacobs of Eco Gardens, Decatur, Georgia, who opened everyone's eyes to the beauty of *Heuchera americana* in his superior selection *H. americana* 'Eco-magnififolia' and numerous *Tiarella* clones—all outstanding plants that he collected in the wild. He has amassed an amazing collection, from which he sells rare plants, especially from the U.S. Southeast and East Asia.

Ted Kipping

Rock gardener and "tree shaper" Ted Kipping of San Francisco has contributed the wonderful selection *Heuchera hirsutissima* 'Santa Rosa' to horticulture.

Luc Klinkhamer

Dutchman Luc Klinkhamer extensively promotes the genus *Heuchera* in The Netherlands and beyond. As a representative of the Dutch auction house CNB-Lisse, Klinkhamer sees to every level of the business from propagation to promotion. He maintained one of the largest *Heuchera* reference collections in the world and offers a Web site, where he lists cultivars and evaluations from his garden.

Luc Klinkhamer.

Marcel LePiniec

Marcel LePiniec worked as a nurseryman, propagator, and plant explorer, at Mayfair, the rock garden nursery he founded in 1924. He later moved to Oregon, where he crossed 'Brizoides' and *Heuchera hallii* to create 'Mayfair', a rock garden cutie. As a founding member of the American Rock Garden Society, he pointed out the benefits of *H. hallii* and the other montane species of *Heuchera* in the rock garden.

Dick Lighty

From his position as curator at the Mt. Cuba Center for the Study of Piedmont Flora in Greenville, Delaware, Dick Lighty introduced some of the toughest landscape heucheras, including such great selections as *Heuchera americana* 'Bartram' and *H. americana* 'Garnet'.

Parker Lewis Little

Parker Lewis Little has also contributed a whole series of *Heuchera americana* selections from the wild. These plants commonly have the prefix "Little's."

Bart O'Brien

Bart O'Brien, director of horticulture at the Rancho Santa Ana Botanic Garden, is another heuchera hero for his extensive work on romantic designs and installation plantings that incorporate heucheras. He is a specialist on California plants and has been the greatest promoter of the hybrid heucheras (*Heuchera maxima* × *H. sanguinea*) created by Lee W. Lenz.

Charles Oliver

The Primrose Path, located in southwestern Pennsylvania, started out as a retail mail-order nursery in 1985 and the following year produced its first small catalog of common field-grown border perennials. Over the next few years the nursery gradually found its niche as a supplier of less readily available perennials for the knowledgeable grower, with an emphasis on native woodland shade plants.

As Charles Oliver became more involved with selecting and breeding native plants, especially in *Heuchera*, *Tiarella*, and *Phlox*, the specialty of The Primrose Path became the yearly introduction of new cultivars of these genera. In 1995 Charles and his wife, Martha, with the help of Regina Birchem, a developmental biologist with experience in the tissue culture of pines, began to micropropagate Primrose Path selections in their new laboratory at the

Charles Oliver.

nursery. This lab was an especial necessity for their new wholesale business, which required far greater quantities than did retail.

Charles Oliver encountered the robust eastern species *Heuchera pubescens* in the mid 1980s in the shale barrens of West Virginia. He grew some plants from wild-collected seed and planted a seedling with conspicuously white-mottled leaves (he called it 'Marble-leaf') in a stock bed next to *H. sanguinea* 'White Cloud'. Seed collected from this *H. pubescens* individual produced a range of obvious hybrids, but the best individual had white-marked leaves and large white flowers. As it turned out, it also had the vigor and drought-tolerance of the *H. pubescens* selection. This 'White Marble' (as it was introduced in 1995) demonstrated to Oliver the tremendous potential for breeding and selection within the genus.

At about this time, Nancy Goodwin introduced 'Montrose Ruby', and Oliver crossed this exceptionally handsome and vigorous plant with his 'White Marble' to produce 'Quilter's Joy'. Repeated backcrosses and crosses of this gene combination yielded other cultivars, adding another range of hybrids—most notably 'Regina', 'Harmonic Convergence', and 'Silver Scrolls'—to Primrose Path's cultivar list.

A second breeding line emerged with the Rocky Mountain montane species *Heuchera pulchella* and *H. hallii*, which were utilized in the early 1990s to produce a range of smaller, attractively proportioned plants, the Miniature Hybrids (later called the San Pico Hybrids). Crosses between the best one of these, 'San Pico Rosita', and the larger burgundy- and silver-leaved forms of the first breeding line yielded the Petite series, which hybrids are smaller plants of an attractive, more compact habit with silver-marked foliage and showy flowers on 10- to 16-inch spikes; 'Petite Marbled Burgundy' and 'Petite Pearl Fairy' are two of the best known of this group.

The closely related native genus *Tiarella* continued to be an important part of the breeding program at The Primrose Path. Starting in the late 1980s, Oliver introduced *Tiarella* hybrids using the eastern species *T. cordifolia* var. *cordifolia* and *T. wherryi* (which he knew as *T. cordifolia* var. *collina*), the forms of which show great diversity in foliage, inflorescence, growth habit, coloration, and shape. When these were crossed with the western species *T. trifoliata* and *T. unifoliata*, the results were stunning. The new hybrids incorporated many traits, and it was then a matter of selecting appealing characteristics. Oliver has selected for showy flowers, maroon leaf markings, and lobed and cut-leaf shapes. The best-known tiarellas of this breeding program are the hybrids 'Tiger Stripe', 'Elizabeth Oliver', and 'Arpeggio'.

An intergeneric hybrid between *Heuchera* and *Tiarella*, ×*Heucherella* 'Bridget Bloom', made by Bressingham master Alan Bloom and introduced by Blooms of Bressingham, had been in the trade since the 1950s. Early on in the Primrose Path breeding program, Oliver decided to duplicate and, if possible, improve upon this cross. The ×*Heucherella* hybrids 'Pink Frost' and 'Snow White' were introduced by Primrose Path (as 'Tinian Pink' and 'Tinian White') in the late 1980s, and, after extensive trialing, heucherellas such as 'Checkered White', 'Quicksilver', and 'Pearl Shadows' followed. The jury is in, and the verdict is that Oliver has wonderfully improved the lot of ×*Heucherella*. Interest in these exciting foamy bells has been significant. Few plants do as well in a reasonably moist, shady woodland setting.

Current *Heuchera* breeding work at The Primrose Path concentrates on combining the large, intensely colored flowers of the best green-leaved forms with the showy purple and silver foliage of recent introductions. Oliver is using *H. villosa* in several more modern forms, adding a soft pubescence to a plant's texture. While Oliver uses his artist's eye in the aesthetic of breeding, he never forgets his horticulturist's senses, always selecting for vigor and hardiness.

The nursery continues to introduce new selections of *Tiarella* and ×*Heuch-*

erella and also works with the contract propagation of its selections by other growers. Charles Oliver keeps his hand in all aspects of the operation, and The Primrose Path remains a small, family-run business.

Piet Oudolf

A designer of world renown, Dutch plantsman and plant breeder Piet Oudolf has done much to promote the inclusion of modern *Heuchera* hybrids, including his own 'Pewter Moon', in the landscape.

Mary Ramsdale

Mary Ramsdale held the NCCPG National Plant Collection of *Heuchera* in England for many years (Bryan Russell, head gardener, maintains the collection for the current holder at the Gilbert Country House, sited at Cliffe, Devon). Her introductions include 'Alison', 'David', 'Rachel', and 'Winkfield'.

Mary Ramsdale.

Wayne Roderick

Noted plantsman Wayne Roderick, another California icon, was master of all things bulbous and Californian. Several of his selections of *Heuchera micrantha* have lent germplasm to current dainty-flowered forms.

M. Nevin Smith

M. Nevin Smith, the heart of Suncrest Nurseries in Watsonville, has been instrumental in the promotion of several excellent selections to the California scene.

Jan Spruyt

Belgian nurseryman Jan Spruyt, owner of Spruyt Nursery in Buggenhout, has introduced several *Heuchera villosa* varieties, beginning in the late 1990s.

Jan van den Top

Dutch breeder Jan van den Top introduced 'Silver Indiana' and 'Beauty Colour' to Holland's wholesale nursery trade in the late 1990s.

Aart Wijnhout

Dutch nurseryman Aart Wijnhout maintained Luc Klinkhamer's trial gardens and has been a liaison between Klinkhamer and distributors like Witteman, B.V., in Holland. His nursery is now closed.

Terra Nova Nurseries

"Hortiholic" Dan Heims has been involved in horticulture since 1973, in particular with the breeding of heucheras. Everyone associates his name, and that of Terra Nova Nurseries, with modern hybrid heucheras. Dan himself tells the tale:

"I've had a lifelong love affair with foliage and variegated plants (my passion for variegation led to my forming, along with fellow hortiholic James Waddick, the variegated plant freaks society known as ABG, 'Anything But Green'), so it's no wonder I fell for the evergreen leaves and shimmering jewel tones of heucheras. And for almost as long, I've engaged in a hobby I call 'sport fishing': wandering through large nurseries looking for sports—a mutant variation, the rare variegated branch or leaf that can be found in a large growing range. One such find from my sport fishing in a retail nursery was a [*Heuchera sanguinea*] with bright cerise flowers and brilliantly variegated foliage, which I subsequently named 'Snow Storm'. In 1988, at the Perennial Plant Association's convention in Portland, Oregon, I carried the leaves and flowers of this plant around in a ziplock bag—a tradition I've kept up, except for newer plants! Two nurserymen went bonkers—Mark Zilis of T & Z Laboratories and Rod Richards of Richalps Nursery in the U.K. By day's end, contracts and distribution rights were set—and the stage was too, for *Heuchera*. To be kind, T & Z failed, but Richalps did a bang-up launch of 'Snow Storm' to the British trade, eventually selling hundreds of thousands of plants.

"Working with *Heuchera americana*, *H. micrantha*, and *H. cylindrica*, I established the base of all my future hybrids with the Splash series and the Veil series, principally 'Pewter Veil'. Working with Randy Burr of B & B Laboratories (a tissue-culture laboratory in Mt. Vernon, Washington), I was able to promote a small list of unusual plants, specializing in *Heuchera*. By the time I joined forces with microbiologist Ken Brown to form Terra Nova Nurseries in 1992, more than a million plants of [*H. sanguinea*] 'Snow Storm' had been sold, and the seed money for Terra Nova Nurseries was set.

"We set up a hood (funky yet functional—and absolutely necessary for tissue-culture work) and a few lights in Ken's home and erected a modest 10-by 30-foot greenhouse to house stock plants and allow controlled breeding. In 1993 we outgrew this area and built a lab from scratch in Ken's backyard. We then rented an 18- by 40-foot dungeon—the windowless basement of an alternative bookstore—for a growing area. Now we needed more space for growing and trialing, so we leased land and procured care from Eric and Cheri Siegmund of Cedarglen Greenhouses in Boring, Oregon (these were the trials that produced 'Amethyst Myst' and 'Plum Pudding') and had a brief stint at Paul Iwasaki's Riverview Greenhouses in Wilsonville."

And the rest is history! Ken and Dan, both of whom were working two jobs at the time, suddenly had to find property with water rights. Fortunately they turned up some dilapidated greenhouses with excellent water in the Canby area, and they have not had to move since. From an initial two and a half acres of land, the Terra Nova operation now spreads over fifteen acres, with one acre in hybridizing trials, over 100,000 square feet under glass, and nearly five acres devoted to research and development.

In 1997 Dan and Ken launched a Web site and began conducting massive trials on *Pulmonaria* (eleven hundred different) and *Tiarella* (three thousand different). By 1998 they had conquered the "ugly flower" syndrome associated with *Heuchera* by introducing hybrids like 'Cherries Jubilee' and 'Ebony and

Ivory'; and their work with *Tiarella* had produced such intergeneric hybrids as ×*Heucherella* 'Silver Streak' and ×*H*. 'Viking Ship'. In 1998 they also began their polyploidy project. Bruce Stermer led the research with Dan's input and direction on varieties; Harini Korlipara came on board in 2000 and carried on the tradition. Other principals in the Terra Nova breeding program include Gary Gossett (since 1999) and Janet Egger, a former Goldsmith Seeds breeder (since late 2000).

Trips around the world have provided extensive new material for breeding as well as some fabulous contacts in the industry. Terra Nova also promotes other breeders' work (Dan was impressed with the work of Charles Oliver and began selling a few of his best plants in the mid 1990s) and raises royalties for their business friends. Ken Brown accomplishes the impossible missions that all nurseries present and has done an immense amount to assure Terra Nova's success. Terra Nova Nurseries now has more than fifty hardworking employees and has introduced more than 450 new varieties to North American horticulture, including these heucheras and heucherellas:

Heuchera 'Amber Waves' PP13348 00
Heuchera 'Amethyst Myst' 96
Heuchera 'Appleblossom' 95
Heuchera 'Autumn Haze' PP12160 99
Heuchera 'Black Beauty' PP13288 01
Heuchera 'Bronze Beacon' 97
Heuchera 'Burgundy Frost' 93
Heuchera 'Can Can' 96
Heuchera 'Cappuccino' 96
Heuchera 'Carousel' 95
Heuchera 'Cascade Dawn' 94
Heuchera 'Cathedral Windows' 97
Heuchera 'Champagne Bubbles'
    PP11259 98
Heuchera 'Cherries Jubilee' PP11377 98
Heuchera 'Chocolate Ruffles' PP8965
    94
Heuchera 'Chocolate Veil' 94
Heuchera 'City Lights' PPAF 04
Heuchera 'Ebony and Ivory' PP11380
    97

Heuchera 'Emerald Veil' 95
Heuchera 'Fandango' PPAF PVR 05
Heuchera 'Fireworks' PP11376 98
Heuchera 'Florist's Choice' PP13151 00
Heuchera 'French Velvet' 99
Heuchera 'Geisha's Fan' PPAF 00
Heuchera 'Green Spice' 93
Heuchera 'Gypsy Dancer' PPAF 04
Heuchera 'High Society' 97
Heuchera 'Hollywood' PPAF PVR 05
Heuchera 'Jack Frost' 95
Heuchera 'Lace Ruffles' 94
Heuchera 'Lime Rickey' PPAF 04
Heuchera 'Magic Wand' PP11390 97
Heuchera 'Mardi Gras' 98
Heuchera 'Marmalade' PPAF 04
Heuchera micrantha 'Krinkles' 94
Heuchera micrantha 'Ruffles' 91
Heuchera 'Mint Frost' 97
Heuchera 'Obsidian' PPAF 02
Heuchera 'Peach Flambé' PPAF PVR 05

Heuchera 'Persian Carpet' 95

Heuchera 'Pewter Veil' PP8984 92

Heuchera 'Pink Lipstick' PPAF 04

Heuchera 'Plum Pudding' 96

Heuchera 'Purple Petticoats' 97

Heuchera 'Purple Sails' 97

Heuchera 'Regal Robe' 97

Heuchera 'Ring of Fire' 95

Heuchera 'Ruby Ruffles' 95

Heuchera 'Ruby Veil' 91

Heuchera sanguinea 'Cherry Splash' 94

Heuchera sanguinea 'Coral Splash' 94

Heuchera sanguinea 'Fairy Cups' 95 (Plate 72)

Heuchera sanguinea 'Frosty' 95

Heuchera sanguinea 'Gold Dust' 98

Heuchera sanguinea 'Snow Storm' 89

Heuchera sanguinea 'Spangles' 96 (Plate 77)

Heuchera sanguinea 'Splish Splash' 96

Heuchera 'Sashay' 98

Heuchera 'Shamrock' 00

Heuchera 'Silver Shadows' 97

Heuchera 'Silver Veil' 92

Heuchera 'Smokey Rose' 97

Heuchera 'Sparkling Burgundy' PPAF PVR 05

Heuchera 'Starry Night' PPAF PVR 05

Heuchera 'Stormy Seas' 96

Heuchera 'Strawberry Candy' PP12195 99

Heuchera 'Strawberry Swirl' 96

Heuchera 'Tango' PPAF PVR 05

Heuchera 'Veil of Passion' PP12166 99

Heuchera 'Velvet Night' 95

Heuchera 'Vesuvius' PP13215 00

Heuchera 'Whirlwind' 98

Heuchera 'White Spires' 97

×*Heucherella* 'Birthday Cake' PPAF 04 (Plate 100)

×*Heucherella* 'Burnished Bronze' PP12159 99

×*Heucherella* 'Chocolate Lace' PP13701 01

×*Heucherella* 'Cinnamon Bear' 99

×*Heucherella* 'Cranberry Ice' 99

×*Heucherella* 'Crimson Clouds' 95

×*Heucherella* 'Dayglow Pink' PP12164 99

×*Heucherella* 'Earth Angel' 97

×*Heucherella* 'Kimono' PP12154 99

×*Heucherella* 'Party Time' PPAF 04 (Plate 107)

×*Heucherella* 'Silver Streak' 97

×*Heucherella* 'Stoplight' PPAF 04

×*Heucherella* 'Sunspot' PPAF 02

×*Heucherella* 'Viking Ship' PP12029 97

As you can see, heucheras have had quite a turn in botanical history, and there is no doubt that *Heuchera*'s story is incomplete, as breakthrough plants hit the commercial scene nearly every year. Move on as we explore more of this fascinating genus . . .

CHAPTER 5

Heuchera Cultivars

The people described in the preceding chapter and others have produced a plethora of cultivars, or named clones—both hybrids and selections of wild species. In the A-to-Z list that follows, we've tried to identify the introducer of each cultivar and the date of the cultivar's release, as well as to describe some of its distinctive characteristics and lineage.

'Absi' PP8858 (Blooms 1997, aka Bressingham Bronze).
This clonal selection of *H. villosa* f. *purpurea* 'Palace Purple' has dark bronze-purple leaves that hold their color longer than most. Cream flowers are not distinctive. Does not burn as badly as poor seed strains of 'Palace Purple'.

'Adriana' (Wijnhout 1999).
Dutch nurseryman Aart Wijnhout did an open-pollinated planting, derived from Terra Nova varieties, from which he selected this red-flowered form. Flower spikes are 24 inches tall. Blooms in early May.

'Alan Davidson' (NCCPG National Collection).
No information from the collection holder.

'Alison' (Ramsdale) (NCCPG National Collection).
Named for Mary Ramsdale's daughter. No information from the collection holder.

'Amber Waves' (Terra Nova 2000).
A sport out of 'Whirlwind'. The light, rose-colored flowers are secondary to the breakthrough amber-gold color of its ruffled foliage, which one designer hailed as the "new neutral." Morning sun works best to maintain the color and prevent any possible leaf scorch in the afternoon. Not as cold hardy or vigorous as many from this line. Plates 1 and 2.

americana **'Bruine Nerving'** (Spruyt / BVBA 1998).
Brown-purple foliage has orangey brown interveins. The underside of leaves is a light green. Medium-sized leaves and 28-inch spikes of insignificant greenish white flowers.

americana **'Dale's Strain'** (Hendricks 1988, aka 'Silver Selection').
This should not be called "Dale's Selection," although that is an understandable mistake considering its history. Named as a grex (defined by Roy Davidson as "a flock or population, a gathering" and by the International Botanical Congress [1950] as "a group of hybrids originating from the same parents but whose individuals vary in appearance") of americana seedlings, mostly green or light bronze, smooth, and lightly silvered. The "Dale" referred to is Dale Hendricks, owner of North Creek Nurseries in southeastern Pennsylvania. Hendricks relates how he found this important plant: "I selected it from a wild population in the mountains of southwest North Carolina in '85 or '86. It was the silver-blue highlights that caught our eye. There was no bronze in the original plants—they freely hybridize and it's tough to keep the pure strain when one has lots of other heucheras around. I grew it first at Greenleaf [Nurseries] as 'Silver Selection'. It remained [so named] until '88 or '89, maybe '90, when the Holbrook catalog came out and Allen "The Bushmeister" Bush introduced it to the wider world as 'Dale's Strain'." Hendricks continues to sell it as 'Silver Selection', and any listing for *H. micrantha* 'Dale' is most likely a misnomer of *H. americana* 'Dale's Strain'. This strain is very drought- and shade-tolerant and selections were used as a base for the early Terra Nova cultivars 'Pewter Veil' and 'Ruby Veil'.

americana **'Eco-magnififolia'** (Jacobs 1994).
A wild selection from the Georgia mountains showing great silvering and blood-red veins in spring; the leaf color fades to a mottled green. Under the right conditions of frost, a bright coral rim will adorn the leaves in winter. Flowers are small and green. Newer plants with superior venation that would appear to owe much (if not all!) of their heritage to this cultivar are 'Diana Clare' and 'Beauty Colour'. Terra Nova used it as a foundation plant for the superb 'Green Spice'. Plate 5.

americana **'Garnet'** (Lighty 1992).
Dick Lighty of the Mt. Cuba Center for the Study of Piedmont Flora selected

this cultivar for its purple winter coloration. This plant is native to Pennsylvania, with foliage to 8 inches and greenish flowers on stems from 24 to 30 inches. Drought- and shade-tolerant. Another (not necessarily *americana*) 'Garnet' was seen in the 1938 RHS Wisley Trials.

americana 'Harry Hay' AM (Hay 1982).

Large, vigorous, purple-leaved seedling sport of *H. americana* raised by Harry Hay, who grew the seed from the American Rock Garden Society seed exchange of 1981, entry no. 1880. Flower stalks are 30 inches tall, consistent with *H. americana* claims. "Lusty" leaves were the largest in recent trials at RHS Wisley.

americana 'Little's Emerald Maroon' (Little 1999).

An *H. americana* selection by Parker Lewis Little found in Hanover County, Virginia. This plant features gold-tipped, glossy, crinkly foliage of green with maroon veins. Flowers are small and indistinct; flower spikes are 21 inches tall. More sun-tolerant than other types. Blooms in early to mid June.

americana 'Little's Fancy Green' (Little 2000).

An *H. americana* selection by Parker Lewis Little found in Hanover County, Virginia. This plant features green foliage with deeper lobes than the type. Flowers are small, green, and indistinct. Dark flower spikes are 28 inches tall. More sun-tolerant than other types.

americana 'Little's Frost Paint' (Little 1999).

An *H. americana* selection by Parker Lewis Little found in Hanover County, Virginia. This plant features mottled, light green foliage in summer followed by silver foliage with brown-gray venation. Silvery blue finish to the leaves is seen in winter. Flowers are small, green, and indistinct. Flower spikes are 30 inches tall. More sun-tolerant than other types.

americana 'Little's Frosty Gem' (Little 1999).

Another *H. americana* selection by Parker Lewis Little found in Hanover County, Virginia. Said to be, perhaps, an improvement over *H. americana* 'Ecomagnififolia'. This plant features light blue-green, maroon-veined foliage in summer turning mottled silver with maroon-gray veins. Flowers are small, green, and indistinct. Flower spikes are 28 inches tall.

americana **'Little's Summer Treasure'** (Little 1999).
An *H. americana* selection by Parker Lewis Little of Virginia. This plant features dark green, maroon-veined summer foliage followed by purple-green to silver foliage marked by dark gray veins. Indistinct flowers are small and green with pink petals. Flower spikes are 28 inches tall.

americana **'Little's Velvet Bouquet'** (Little 2000).
An *H. americana* selection by Parker Lewis Little of Virginia. This cultivar features metallic purplish silver-gray foliage. Leaf backside is maroon. Similar to 'Montrose Ruby'. Flowers are small, green, and indistinct. Flower spikes grow 23 inches tall. Blooms in mid May to mid June.

americana **'Little's Winter Emerald'** (Little 1999).
Heuchera americana cultivar of Parker Lewis Little of Virginia. This cultivar features green, maroon-veined summer foliage followed by purple-green to silver foliage marked by dark gray veins. Indistinct flowers are small and green with pink petals. Flower spikes grow 23 inches tall. Blooms in mid May to mid June.

americana **'Little's Winter Ice'** (Little 1999).
An *H. americana* cultivar of Parker Lewis Little of Virginia. This plant features silvery-mottled, green-veined summer foliage followed by light green-white foliage marked by green veins. Indistinct flowers are small and green with white petals. Flower spikes grow 14 inches tall in mid May to mid June.

americana **'Little's Winter Treasure'** (Little 2000).
An *H. americana* cultivar of Parker Lewis Little of Virginia. This plant features silvery-mottled, green-veined summer foliage marked by purple veins. Foliage in winter is dark green with a gold-silver overlay. Indistinct flowers are small and green with white petals. Flower spikes grow 22 inches tall in mid May to mid June.

americana **'Picta'.**
Listed in the RHS Horticultural Database as an accepted name, but this is a very dubious claim.

'Amethyst Myst' (Terra Nova 1996).
A sister to 'Plum Pudding'. This shade-lover offers a foliage color that is different from the burgundy tones of earlier hybrids. Noted Canadian garden

writer Marjorie Harris, who kept this cultivar in a terra-cotta pot, called 'Amethyst Myst' "the Queen of all she surveys" come autumn. The glossy-leaved clump can achieve an impressive 24 inches across. Flowers are purple infused white and are not showy. Plate 7.

'Angel's Pink' (Smith 1983).
This floriferous sanguinea hybrid with large, bright pink flowers on 18-inch spikes and mottled foliage was introduced by Suncrest Nurseries of Watsonville, California. Its name refers to Angel Guerzon, a local plant nut, who worked at Wintergreen Nursery with Nevin and then later at Orchard Supply. Seems to have been temporarily lost to cultivation; if you have plants, please contact Nevin Smith at Suncrest Nurseries, postmaster@suncrestnurseries .com, and he will see that it gets reintroduced.

'Annemarie' (Eikholt 1999).
A seedling from sanguinea hybrids tested in Lisse, The Netherlands. Pink flowers sit atop 14-inch spikes over green foliage from May to July.

'Apple Blossom' AM 1938 (Blooms 1938).
A delicate pink with darker tips. Flower spikes are 30 inches tall with a stingy blooming habit. Blooms classifies it as a sanguinea form. Dropped by Blooms and lost to cultivation.

'Appleblossom' (Terra Nova 1995).
One of Terra Nova's earliest introductions, 'Appleblossom' had a good run in New Zealand. White flowers rimmed with pink are carried on tall, 26-inch stalks. Flowers are larger and more teardrop-shaped than *H. sanguinea*, hinting toward some *H. micrantha* parentage. Grows well in full sun and heavier soils. Named without knowledge of Blooms' earlier plant. Plate 8.

'Argus' AM 1924 (Lemoine 1920).
A winner at the RHS Wisley Trials, this large-flowered carmine variety was raised by Lemoine et Fils in Nancy, France.

'Autumn Haze' (Terra Nova 1999).
A hybrid derived from 'French Velvet'. Velvety foliage is tinted with cinnamon and purple. This cultivar has extremely short petioles and superb vena-

tion and form. The rose-tinted flowers are on arching stalks that are up to 20 inches long in spring. An excellent container candidate. Plate 9.

'Baby's Breath' (Chatto / RHS Wisley List) (NCCPG National Collection). No information from the collection holder.

'*Beauty*' (Wijnhout 1999).
Aart Wijnhout selected this cream-flowered form from an open-pollinated planting derived from Terra Nova varieties. Flower spikes are 16 inches tall. Foliage is brown. Blooms from May to September.

'Beauty Colour'.
Nearly identical to *H. americana* 'Eco-magnififolia' in its superior venation, there is much European distribution of this clone. Plate 10.

'Beldex' (Wijnhout 1999).
Aart Wijnhout selected this pink-flowered form from an open-pollinated planting derived from Terra Nova varieties. Flower spikes are 24 inches tall. Foliage is green. Blooms in May and June.

'Benzi' (Wijnhout 1999).
Aart Wijnhout selected this white-flowered form from an open-pollinated planting derived from Terra Nova varieties. Flower spikes are 24 inches tall. Foliage is brown. Blooms in May and June.

'Black Beauty' (Terra Nova 2001).
One of Dan's Top 5, this ruffled beauty has very dark, glossy foliage that seems to catch the light at any angle and glow with a crimson-red. The undersides are the darkest burgundy, and the surface color holds all season long. Flowers are small and cream-colored on elegant, proportional spikes. Best placed in full sun, where its charms can be appreciated. Blooms in June. Plate 11.

'Blackbird' AGM (Witteman 1996).
Aart Wijnhout did an open-pollinated planting, derived from Terra Nova varieties, from which Witteman selected this pink-flowered seed selection. Flower spikes are 20 inches tall. Foliage is brown. Blooms in May and June.

'Black Velvet' (Invalid Name).
Listed only once in the *RHS Plant Finder* by Four Seasons Nursery in the
United Kingdom but not seen in their catalogs.

'Blood Red' PPAF PVR (Terra Nova 2005).
After much work to return a dark red to the palette, the breeders at Terra Nova
have produced a most showy plant. Large, blood-red flowers on 20-inch stalks
over bright green leaves swirled with a silvery white overlay. Small, compact
habit. The foliage mound is 7 inches tall and 12 inches wide.

'Bloom's Variety' AM (Blooms 1930).
A hybrid between *H. sanguinea* 'Trevor Red' and 'Brizoides'. Lost to cultivation. Flowers were said to be twice as big as its 'Brizoides' parent. Warm red
flowers were held on 30-inch spikes from May to July. Originated during the
family's Oakington stay.

'Blushing Bells' (Emery / Santa Barbara Botanic Garden 1989).
An unusual cross of a sanguinea hybrid and a smaller mountain species, originally referred to in SBBG reports as *H. pringlei* (which is now synonymous
with *H. rubescens*). Like its sister 'Dainty Bells', it forms a mat of dense, spreading rosettes. Flower spikes are small with soft pink flowers to 8 inches tall.
Great for borders, troughs, and the rock garden.

'Bouquet Rose' (NCCPG National Collection).
A compact 'Brizoides', hispida foliage, floriferous, hardy.

'Brandon Glow' (Morden 1983) (*H. sanguinea* × *H. richardsonii*).
Henry Marshall bred this extraordinary heuchera at the Morden Research Station. This plant is not only tough but also sports delft-rose flowers on 20-
inch spikes over green foliage. Bloom time is in June.

'Brandon Pink' (Morden 1983) (*H. sanguinea* × *H. richardsonii*).
Another extraordinary result of Henry Marshall's work at the Morden
Research Station. Apparently, the seed of *H. richardsonii* was collected from
northern Alberta near Canada's equivalent of Siberia, the Northwest Territories. This floriferous heuch is northern-tough and sports coral-pink flowers on
20-inch spikes over green foliage. Bloom time is in June.

'Bressingham Blaze' AM 1965 (Blooms 1950).
Flowering spikes to 28 inches support turkey-red flowers over this free-flowering though weak-growing plant. Green foliage. It snagged its Award of Merit for Exhibition when shown by Alan Bloom; it is fully described in the *Journal of the RHS* (1965) 90:484, fig. 226.

'Bressingham Glow' (NCCPG National Collection).
Bryan Russell, keeper of the collection, reports that this is not, as one might expect from the name, an Alan Bloom introduction. No further information available.

Bressingham Hybrids (Blooms 1950).
Selections were made by Alan Bloom and Percy Piper (a Blooms plantsman) of the fifty top plants from more than two thousand open-pollinated heucheras. This wonderful group of hybrids from 'Brizoides', *H. sanguinea*, *H. micrantha*, and *H. americana* crosses provides myriad colors, including pink, red, orange, coral, white, and a brownish red (typical of red × green hybrids). Fascinating variations are always provided by this free-flowering strain, which has remained the most popular seed strain for more than half a century. Plants need to be reselected through time to strengthen the strain.

'Bressingham Spire' (NCCPG National Collection).
Bryan Russell reports that this too is not an Alan Bloom introduction.

'Brizoides' (Lemoine 1897) (*H. sanguinea* × *H. americana* var. *hispida* f. *purpurea*).
We are hereby proposing that this plant be referred to, styled, and spelled out as listed here (although it often seen as ×*brizoides*). It is *not* an intergeneric plant as was originally believed; it is a hybrid, in the accepted fashion of nomenclature, and worthy of its cultivar name as bestowed by the famous French breeder. The reason for the name? The inflorescence resembles that of the ornamental grass *Briza*.

Lemoine et Fils included this historic plant—the first *Heuchera* hybrid offered to the public—in their catalog no. 135 in the fall of 1897, describing it thus: "A plant of absolute rusticity, forming small acaulescent tufts and palmate, dentate leaves that are clear and shiny with a red-bronze color during development and green-bronze during summer. Flowers are on stalks 50–60 cm. and campanulate with a clear carmine-colored rose to carmine tips, with soft white petals and short red stamens." They declared it a hybrid between *H. sanguinea* and *Tiarella purpurea*; it would be at least ten years before Lemoine et Fils realized it was not *T. purpurea* they were dealing with. The first mention of 'Brizoides' in English horticultural literature came in *The Garden* in 1899 (55:86).

The *Heuchera sanguinea* was never in doubt, but much of the confusion carried forth through the years concerning the origin of the seminal 'Brizoides' may be attributed to that fact that ensuing experts simply did not know what other plant they were talking about. The Lemoine catalogs refer to an M. L. Chauré who wrote an article in the *Moniteur d'Horticulture* in 1903 stating with certainty that the other plant in the 'Brizoides' makeup was a tiarella. He was not the first nor was he the last (not knowing the difference in stamen count) to make such a mistake. Around 1906, the Lemoines themselves changed their minds about the tiarella, calling it *H. purpurea*. But both *Tiarella purpurea* and *H. purpurea* were invalid names for nonexistent plants. Later the Lemoines believed they were dealing with *H. richardsonii*, although it was referred to parenthetically as *H. hispida*.

Nomenclatural confusion between *Heuchera richardsonii* and *H. hispida* is understandable when one looks at the taxonomic history: the mix-up had gained significant momentum when Asa Gray reduced *H. richardsonii* to synonymy under *H. hispida* in 1849, and Rydberg added to the muddle when he reclassified *H. richardsonii* as *H. hispida* var. *richardsonii* (Britton 1901). In 1933 Rosendahl et al. claimed they were two different species; Rosendahl himself believed that *hispida* was a variety of *H. americana*. Others believed that *H. americana* var. *hispida* was a natural hybrid between *H. pubescens* and *H. americana*. It was not until 1979 that *hispida* found its true (current) place as a variety of *H. americana* (Wells, Rhodora). Further to the unraveling of this mystery, Émile Lemoine, in a personal letter in May 1939 to William Stearn of the RHS, states that 'Brizoides' derived from "*H. americana* var. *purpurea* and *H. sanguinea*" (Musée d'Ecole, Nancy, France). Or what he *thought* was *H. americana* var. *purpurea*: we can now set the botanical record straight and conclude that f. *purpurea* of *H. americana* var. *hispida*, which purple form is not uncommon, crossed with *H. sanguinea* yielded 'Brizoides'.

Émile Lemoine was personally responsible for most heuchera crosses; he later backcrossed 'Brizoides' with *Heuchera micrantha* to produce 'Gracillima' (see that listing), and in the ensuing years Lemoine et Fils offered many 'Brizoides' and 'Gracillima' cultivars. Members of the Brizoides Group are taller than the sanguinea cultivars; they are often used in the border as feature plants or edgers and as cheerful groundcovers in light woodland and natural garden settings.

The genetic scope of 'Brizoides' formed the basis for much of what Alan Bloom and many others have been doing for the last seventy years. It has had many different forms in horticulture, with dubious names like 'Alba' (next entry) and 'Robusta' (which was seen in catalogs of the 1930s).

Brizoides Group 'Alba'.
This is the white-flowered form with sprays of rose-tinted white flowers to 24 inches. Foliage is a medium-green mound to 6 inches tall.

Brizoides Group 'Perry's Variety' (Perry 1931).
Perry's Hardy Plant Farm's 1933 catalog describes this hybrid as has having an "immense number of wiry branching stems smothered with brilliant crimson flowers." Flower spikes are 24 inches tall, and plants bloom from June to August. Touted (oh so humbly) at the time as "the finest *Heuchera* yet introduced"!

Brizoides Group 'Roi de Violets'.
From neat tufts of olive-green foliage emanate "numerous spikes of rich, ruby-crimson flowers; as the flowers age they assume a distinct flush of violet" (Perry's Hardy Plant Farm 1933 catalog). Eighteen-inch spikes appear from June to August.

'Bronze Beacon' (Terra Nova 1997).
A breakthrough hybrid (involving *H. americana*, *H. sanguinea*, and *H. micrantha*) at the time of its introduction, this heir apparent to 'Palace Passion' has darker leaves and elegant flower spikes to 28 inches with red flowers. Given to Walter's Gardens as an exclusive.

'Brown Coral' (Sahin 1999).
A seedling-derived selection of the 'Pruhoniciana' persuasion, most likely from 'Raspberry Regal'. The Cotswold Garden Flowers catalog described it thus: "A flower arranger's dream, tight upright spikes of brown-coral flowers May to July and later. Compact form, leaves build upon an 8" mound, while flower spikes grow to 24" tall. Easy."

'Brownfinch' (Maureen Iddon 1990) (sport seedling of *H. cylindrica*
'Greenfinch').
Sometimes seen listed as a selection of *H. cylindrica*, this is clearly just a hybrid
with some cylindrica genes. Stiff upright 20-inch stems (courtesy of the *H.
cylindrica* 'Greenfinch' heritage) make it an excellent choice for cuts.

'Burgundy Frost' AGM (Terra Nova 1993).
One of Terra Nova's very early hybrids of *H. americana* and 'Pewter Veil'. Silvered bronze leaves are smaller and tighter than 'Pewter Veil' and fade attractively to new tones through the year. Rare in cultivation.

'Can Can' AGM (Terra Nova 1996) ('Pewter Veil'× 'Ruby Ruffles').
One of the first of the ruffled forms to take on the metallic silvers of 'Pewter
Veil'. Truly different from all the others in that it forms a tight, ruffled mound.
Really stunning as it reflects the morning light. Flowers are a nondescript
cream color. Plate 12.

'Canyon Belle' (Emery / Santa Barbara Botanic Garden 1997) (F_2 *H. elegans* ×
H. sanguinea).
Rich red flowers on 18-inch stalks. Closer in shape and size to its *H. sanguinea*
parent. Leaves are somewhat glossy, and the foliage mounds are 5 inches high
and 12 inches across.

'Canyon Chimes' (Emery / Santa Barbara Botanic Garden 1997) (F_2 'Canyon
Delight' × *H. elegans*).
Cherry-pink flowers on 16-inch stalks. A strong performer.

'Canyon Delight' (Emery / Santa Barbara Botanic Garden 1985) (F_1 *H.
sanguinea* × *H. elegans*).
Good pink coloration on flowers in loose sprays from 14 to 18 inches. Should
be hardier than most in the Canyon series.

'Canyon Duet' (Emery / Santa Barbara Botanic Garden 1997) (F_2 *H. elegans* ×
'Canyon Delight').
One of the strongest growers in the Canyon series and considered by some to
be the best. Plant is very compact and floriferous with dark rose flowers tipped
in white on 12-inch stalks.

'Canyon Melody' (Emery / Santa Barbara Botanic Garden 1997) (F_2 *H. elegans* × 'Canyon Pink').
Twelve-inch stalks of pink flowers arise from a low, 3-inch mound of foliage. Flowers are distinctive: the white petals are exserted from the pink calyces.

'Canyon Pink' (Emery / Santa Barbara Botanic Garden 1985) (F_1 *H. sanguinea* × *H. elegans*).
An excellent compact hybrid with rose-pink flower spikes only 8 inches tall on average. A really prodigious bloomer with a western montane heritage. Plate 13.

'Cappuccino' (Terra Nova 1996) (*H. micrantha* 'Ruffles' × 'Chocolate Ruffles').
Dan describes this new color form of bronze as "espresso with a shot of cream, a warm color to combine with golds and yellows in the garden." Leaves are lightly ruffled and fuzzy. Flowers are not showy. Very sun-tolerant. Plate 14.

'Caramel' (Thierry de Labroye 2005).
A French hybrid of *H. villosa* and possibly 'Amber Waves'. Large, caramel-tinted leaves on a large and vigorous plant. Shy bloomer.

'Carmen' (Blooms 1950).
Bright shows of 20-inch carmine-pink sprays over dark-colored foliage. Spring bloomer. This cultivar does well in containers and in the rock garden, where it has proven to be quite drought-tolerant.

'Carousel' (Terra Nova 1995).
An early *H. micrantha* × *H. sanguinea* hybrid. Foliage is silvered, broad, slightly hairy, and beautifully mounded into an almost birthday cake–like form that somehow reminds Dan of a carousel. Flowers are an attractive red on spikes to 20 inches tall. Rare in cultivation. Plate 15.

'Cascade Dawn' (Terra Nova 1994) ('Emerald Veil' × 'Pewter Veil').
Aptly named—this cultivar's appearance is reminiscent of the early morning sun reflecting off the Northwest's snow-covered Cascade Mountains. Leaves are smooth with charcoal-gray venation. Flowers are not showy. With lavender shading consistent throughout the season, in some years it can surpass its sister, 'Pewter Veil'. Plate 16.

'Cathedral Windows' (Terra Nova 1997) ('Ruby Veil' × 'Velvet Night').
Full, dark leaves show patches of metallic purple on a plant 7 inches high. The color and venation of these leaves reminded Dan of stained glass. Insignificant flowers are on 25-inch stems. Plate 17.

'Champagne Bubbles' (Terra Nova 1998).
A hybrid of *H. americana* and *H. pubescens*. Numerous, tall, upright flowering stems with flowers changing from white to pink. Compact, glossy green foliage. Flowering stems are 30 inches tall on plants 7 inches tall and 16 inches wide. Good in mass plantings. Plate 18.

'Charles Bloom' (Blooms 1985, aka Chablo).
Graceful, wide-arching sprays of soft pink flowers. Named in memory of Alan Bloom's father, an early hybridizer of *Heuchera*. Flowering stems are 20 inches tall; the rosette is 12 inches wide. Green foliage.

'Chatterbox' (Cummings).
A selection of 'Brizoides' that has been around for quite a while, certainly since the 1950s, this cultivar does well in containers and in the rock garden, where it has proven to be quite drought-tolerant. Its rose-pink flowers bloom above the green foliage in May and June. Sporadic rebloom.

'Cherries Jubilee' (Terra Nova 1998) (*H. sanguinea* × 'Palace Passion').
An early breakthrough, combining sanguinea-like light red flowers on warm brown foliage. The foliage has slight ruffling. Great in containers. Small habit. At 16 to 20 inches, flower spikes are not as tall as many. Plate 19.

'Cherry Red' (Invalid Name).
Listed only once (in 1997) in the *RHS Plant Finder* by Beth Chatto Gardens, Ltd., in the United Kingdom, but not seen in their catalogs since.

'Chinook' (Terra Nova 2005).
The breeders of Terra Nova have used tetraploidy to produce plants with stronger, more resistant foliage and larger flowers of greater substance and color. 'Chinook' is one such plant. Derived from 'Fireworks', which has proven to be an excellent reblooming workhorse, 'Chinook' is even better. Leaves are glossy brown and ruffled. The very large flowers range from a light to a dark

salmon, depending on sun exposure. It prefers a full-sun location. Spread is 14 inches wide, with flower stalks as tall. Blooms May through August. Plate 20.

'Chiqui' (George Schenk 1989) (*H. sanguinea* × *H. cylindrica*).
It has amazing constitution and vigor, blooming longer than many cultivars. Strong 28-inch spikes of bright pink flowers burst forth to create a cotton candy effect. The sturdy, nonflopping stems arise from a neat rosette of compact foliage. Very "cheeky" and highly recommended. Plate 21.

'Chocolate Ruffles' (Terra Nova 1994) (*H. micrantha* 'Ruffles' × 'Ruby Veil').
One of America's and Europe's favorites and a big reason for the rise in the popularity of the genus *Heuchera*. Incredibly ruffled leaves, chocolate on the top, burgundy on the bottom. The most robust foliage of hybrid heucheras, generally reaching 15 inches in height. Thousands of small purplish flowers on strong 30-inch purple spikes. It's a really fine cultivar for the southern United States. Plates 22 and 23.

'Chocolate Veil' AGM (Terra Nova 1994).
An *H. americana* cross with beautiful smooth chocolate-black leaves up to 9 inches across. Foliage has purple highlights. Nondescript whitish flowers. Plate 24.

'Chocolate White' (Wijnhout 1999).
Aart Wijnhout selected this cream-flowered form from an open-pollinated planting derived from Terra Nova varieties. Flower spikes are 16 inches tall. Foliage is brown. Blooms in June and July.

'Cinde' (Witteman 1996).
Aart Wijnhout did an open-pollinated planting, derived from Terra Nova varieties, from which Witteman selected this red-flowered form. Flower spikes are 28 inches tall. Foliage is green with white variegation. Blooms from May to August.

'City Lights' (Terra Nova 2004).
A vigorous bronze-leaved hybrid (with *H. duranii*) with luminous cream-yellow flowers—a flower-color breakthrough—over chocolate leaves. The flower spikes stand out not only for their sheer number but also because on

each spike the flowers are symmetrically layered. Plants are 12 inches wide with flower spikes to 30 inches. Plate 25.

'Claudia' (Wijnhout 1999).

Aart Wijnhout selected this red-flowered form from an open-pollinated planting derived from Terra Nova varieties. Flower spikes are 14 inches tall. Foliage is green. Blooms from May to July.

'Color Dream' (van den Top 2005).

A sport of 'Beauty Colour', this has much more silvering than its parent and whitish flowers. Blooms in June and July with 16-inch flower spikes. Red edges on some leaves in winter, as is characteristic of this group.

'Constance' (Betty Ann Addison 1996).

A lovely, petite, miniature hybrid with short (6-inch) spikes of bicolored (pink and white) flowers. Seems to languish somewhat in normal garden conditions, suggesting that it has western montane genes and therefore it desires oxygen around its roots. Best suited to troughs and rock gardens with perfect drainage. This has proven quite hardy to Zone 5 as long as drainage concerns are addressed.

'Coral Bouquet' (Primrose Path 1997) ('Brizoides' × *H. cylindrica* var. *alpina*).

A heuchera of compact proportions with an inflorescence anywhere from 18 to 24 inches. Very large, splendid coral blooms four times the size of any "normal" heuchera. Flowers are described in the Primrose Path catalog as having, "cattail-shaped inflorescences." Flowers are densely clustered, and the plant habit is very neat. Some light silver patterning on the leaves. Must have good drainage.

'Coral Cloud' (Blooms 1932).

'Brizoides' selection with crinkly foliage and a shiny finish. Coral-red flowers are larger and taller (30 inches) than 'Gracillima'.

'Corallion' AM 1938 (Blooms 1932).

A large-flowered, free-flowering form with mid-pink blooms. Thought to be lost to cultivation until Mary Ramsdale presented the RHS Wisley Trials with what she believed was the true form.

'Countess of Romney' (Blooms 1950, aka 'Lady Romney').
This plant was chosen by her Ladyship herself. It has pale pink "Empire Rose" flowers on 24-inch "light green, tinged brown" flower spikes. Blooms later dropped it. Reports say it had well-marbled foliage to 8 inches and a vigorous, loose habit. Alan Bloom himself crossed off 'Lady Romney' and entered 'Countess of Romney' on the 1954 RHS Wisley Trials form. Obviously, the Countess was not a mere Lady.

'Crème Brûlée' (Terra Nova 2005).
This plant was chosen by Proven Winners to star in their Dolce series of plants, each with the name of a dessert. 'Crème Brûlée' is a large-leaved plant with coppery foliage that fades slightly to a cream with a darker amber edge. Leaves are purpled on the back. Flowers are not distinctive. The foliage mound measures up to 12 inches high and 24 inches wide, with flower stalks to 22 inches. Plate 26.

'Crimson Curls' (Brown 2000) (seed selection from 'Chocolate Ruffles').
Foot-tall clumps spread to 2 feet. Foliage is curly, less so than 'Whirlwind' but more so than 'Chocolate Ruffles', which plant Dan brought to Ray Brown (of Plantworld, a U.K. seed company) in the early 1990s. Purple foliage color fades badly by late summer but apparently holds up very nicely in the English winters.

'Crispy Curly' (Brown 1999).
A ruffled strain, carried by Warren Hills Nursery in Leicester, United Kingdom, said to have "parsley-like foliage and greenish-white flowers." Spikes are 24 inches tall, and the plant is 12 inches wide. The betting says that this strain is a seedling selection derived from *H. micrantha* 'Ruffles'. Handled by B & T World Seeds.

'Crown Jewel' (Terra Nova / Clifford's 1998).
A mutation of 'Can Can' but without the rosy overlay. It is a markedly more yellow-tinted plant yet maintains a silvery sheen. The ruffling is identical to 'Can Can'. Evolved as a single tissue-culture sport, it was then increased by Clifford's Perennial and Vine at a lab in Florida.

***cylindrica* 'Chartreuse'** (1999).
An open-pollinated selection. Mike Grant, botanist at RHS Wisley, reports,

"Les Jardins de John [John Hoyland's French nursery, recently reestablished in the United Kingdom as Pioneer Nurseries] have the following description of *H. cylindrica* 'Chartreuse': flowering in July, 24 inches by 14 inches, 'boutons roses qui s'ouvrent en clochettes vertes,' which, on translation, we think means 'pink buds open to little green bells.'"

cylindrica **'Greenfinch'** (Blooms 1950, aka 'Gruenfink').
A rugged plant and certainly one of the finest selections of *H. cylindrica*, with chartreuse flowers of moderate size on stiff upright stalks, 16 to 26 inches in height. The foliage is highly silvered and attractive. It is drought-tolerant and partial to sun. Also used as a cut flower—a staple for flower arrangers. Makes a good groundcover in shady areas and sets off showier plants.

cylindrica **'Wingwell Anna'** (Wingwell Nursery 1990).
Selected seedling of *H. cylindrica* from seed obtained by the nursery through the Hardy Plant Society seed exchange. Silver-marbled leaves and salmon-pink flowers on a plant of neat habit (which one would expect of an *H. cylindrica* selection). First exhibited at the Lincoln Show in England in 1991.

'Dainty' (Blooms 1951).
A small-flowered, very free-flowering form with mid-pink blooms on 24-inch stalks.

'Dainty Bells' (Emery / Santa Barbara Botanic Garden 1989).
Cross between a hybrid of *H. sanguinea* and *H. hirsutissima*, the shaggy-hair alumroot. Like 'Blushing Bells', it forms a mat of dense, spreading rosettes. Flower spikes are small, with rose-pink flowers to 8 inches tall.

'Daisy Mill' (NCCPG National Collection).
Originally acquired from Mary Ramsdale. Bryan Russell, keeper of the collection, says that the foliage is similar to 'Strawberry Swirl'; he has yet to see the flowers, but he thinks it is an old Irish variety.

'Damask' (Blooms 1954) (NCCPG National Collection).
Received by the collection in 1981, this hybrid has widely expanded crimson blooms on 18-inch sprays in early June. The foliage mound is 6 inches tall, medium-green.

'Daniels' Giant Scarlet' (Daniels 1934).
Originally raised by Frank Neave of Lingwood and introduced by the Daniels Brothers of Norwich. This was to be an improvement of 'Coccinea', with taller and larger flowers over a stronger plant. The foliage mound is 6 inches tall, and leaves are colored a dark green. The plant has a compact habit. Flowers are a rich scarlet on 24-inch stalks and are considered a good cut.

'Dappled Barbara' (Brown 2000).
This seedling mutation offers variegated foliage on swirled leaves. Flowers are not showy. Introduced by Bob Brown, one of the world's most English gentlemen, and named for the Cotswold Garden Flowers employee who found it.

'Dark Delight' (Smith 1975).
This plant was named by Nevin Smith and preceded the introduction of *H. villosa* f. *purpurea* 'Palace Purple' by five years, but the species involved are unknown. It was a gift from plant explorer Bill Baker, offered under the name "spp. Mexican." The small white flowers are tinged pink and are produced on dark red stems in summer; flower stalk height is 12 inches (too small for *H. americana*). The plant forms tight clumps, with rosettes of broadly lobed, nearly flat leaves, often over 3 inches across; they are more distinctly bicolored than those of 'Palace Purple', and more green above. Leaves have a lovely satiny sheen, smoother and less velvety than those of 'Palace Purple'.

'David' (Ramsdale 1994).
Another cross between *H. villosa* f. *purpurea* 'Palace Purple' and a white-flowered selection of a sanguinea hybrid thought to be 'Sunset'. It has a very strong, spreading habit with large bronze-green leaves and late summer blooms to 30 inches set off by prominent bracts. Seems fine in full sun. Much larger and more vigorous than 'Rachel', its sister seedling, with very good winter foliage in maritime climes. Mary Ramsdale named this hybrid for her son. Plate 28.

'Diana Clare' (Brown 1999).
Large burgundy leaves can develop coral edges; 20-inch spikes hold small, nonshowy red flowers, which bloom for a long period, June to October.

'Dingle Amber' (Invalid Name).
Not offered since 1991, this is a chance seedling of *H. villosa* f. *purpurea* 'Palace

Purple' with orangey brown foliage and the typical creamy white flowers of 'Palace Purple'. From the Dingle Nursery in the United Kingdom.

'Dingle Mint Chocolate' (Invalid Name).
Not seen since 1991, this chance seedling of *H. villosa* f. *purpurea* 'Palace Purple' has brown foliage edged in lime-green in the spring and the typical creamy white flowers of 'Palace Purple'. Green edge fades by midsummer. From the Dingle Nursery in the United Kingdom.

'Duchess' (NCCPG National Collection).
No information from the collection holder.

'Ebony and Ivory' (Terra Nova 1997) (*H. micrantha* 'Ruffles' × black-leaved seedling).
Large ivory flowers bloom over ruffled, light charcoal foliage. In less light, the leaves of this extremely sun-proof form will develop silver streaking. This cultivar is becoming very popular in Europe thanks to the effort of Holland's Henk Goeijers. In Luc Klinkhamer's trials in 1999, it was the only heuch of three hundred to receive a top rating of 4. Plate 29.

'Eden's Aurora' (de Vroomen 1999).
Aart Wijnhout did an open-pollinated planting, derived from Terra Nova varieties, from which Jac de Vroomen selected this heuchera. Flowers, billed as yellow, are rather a green shade of cream. Spikes are 24 inches tall over green foliage. This selection did rather poorly in Oregon in the 2000 Terra Nova Trials.

'Eden's Joy' (de Vroomen 1999).
Aart Wijnhout did an open-pollinated planting, derived from Terra Nova varieties, from which Jac de Vroomen selected this heuchera. Flowers are a green shade of cream. Spikes are 24 inches tall over green foliage. Blooms in May and June.

'Eden's Mystery' (de Vroomen 1999).
Aart Wijnhout did an open-pollinated planting, derived from Terra Nova varieties, from which Jac de Vroomen selected this heuchera. Flowers are cream-colored. Spikes are 16 inches tall over brown foliage. Said to be the best of the Eden series and is now the only one de Vroomen offers. Blooms in June and July.

'Eden's Shine' (de Vroomen 1999).
Another seed selection from an open-pollinated group of Terra Nova cultivars. One of the darkest heuchera forms with reddish burgundy leaves, it transforms itself to a dark purple as the season progresses. Flowers are a creamy pink color on 16-inch spikes.

'Edge Hall' (Wolley-Dod 1902, aka 'Edge Hybrid') (*H. sanguinea* × *H. cylindrica*).
Edge Hall was the home and nursery of Rev. Charles Wolley-Dod (1826–1904). Available in the Blooms catalog in the 1930s, this sanguinea hybrid was charmingly listed as having "rather dull pink flowers on short spikes." The shape of the blossoms indicates the cylindrica parentage. The form now circulating might, in fact, be a selection of 'Sancyl' made by Bloom in the 1930s and simply renamed. This cultivar does well in containers and in the rock garden, where it has proven to be quite drought-tolerant.

elegans **'Bella Blanca'** (Rancho Santa Ana Botanic Garden 1999).
A mat-forming albino introduction that gives rise to white-flowered spikes 4 to 8 inches above the foliage. Bart O'Brien has this report: "'Bella Blanca' is a selection of *Heuchera elegans*, direct from the wild. It is an albino form collected by me in the San Gabriel Mountains in 1994. . . . It is very hardy, to at least Sunset zone 3 (and maybe even lower) (USDA Zone 5)." Great for containers and rock gardens.

'Elvira' (Wijnhout 1997).
Sixteen-inch spikes of pink flowers over green leaves. Blooms in May.

'Emerald Veil' (Terra Nova 1995).
An early hybrid selection of *H. americana* 'Dale's Strain' and a vintage Terra Nova plant. Leaves have a splendid dark green velvety sheen and are overlaid with silvery netting. Flowers are not showy. 'Mint Frost' was selected to supersede this beauty, which was never in wide distribution.

'Emperor's New Clothes' (Sahin 2002).
A mix of open-pollinated seed with (of course) various colors, shapes, and sizes of leaves and different heights and finishes of flowers. Kees Sahin is a Dutch seedsman. Jelitto offers a similar blend.

'Fandango' (Terra Nova 2005).
Very free-flowering form with pink wand-type flowers on short stalks. Small habit with well-veiled, ruffled leaves. Differs from 'Gypsy Dancer' as the leaves are ruffled, the flower stalks much shorter and tighter, and the flowers darker. One of the Dance series from Terra Nova. Plate 30.

'Fantaisie' (Lemoine 1902).
A 'Brizoides' selection and the first heuchera offered as having marbled bronze foliage as a selling feature. Clear green flowers were tipped in bronze and stood on strong stalks to 30 inches.

'Feuerlohe' (Raging Flames) (Klose 1978).
From German plantsman Heinz Klose came this cultivar with green leaves and vivid red flowers on 20-inch stalks.

'Firebird' HC 1955 (Blooms 1953).
Very free-flowering 14-inch spikes of bright crimson blooms over 8-inch mounds of foliage. This cultivar does well in containers and in the rock garden, where it has proven to be quite drought-tolerant.

'Fire in the Mist' (McCarrick 2000).
The owners of Spring Thyme Nursery in Lakeport, California, introduced this variegated *H. sanguinea* through Pride of Place Plants of Sidney, British Columbia. The flowers are a warmer shade of red than the cerise of *H. sanguinea* 'Snow Storm'. The foliage's markings are fairly similar to those of *H. sanguinea* 'Splish Splash' and *H. sanguinea* 'Cherry Splash'. Flower spikes top out at 14 inches.

'Fireworks' AGM (Terra Nova 1998).
Sibling to 'Ebony and Ivory' and 'Cherries Jubilee', 'Fireworks' can make a smashing and long-lasting effect en masse. An explosive display of soft coral flowers is set off over a 6-inch-tall mound of lightly ruffled bronze leaves. Flowers over a very long period and often reblooms. It also blooms well in the shade, where the veiling of the foliage is more pronounced. Plate 31.

'Flambeau' (Lemoine 1901).
The first 'Brizoides' cultivar listed by Lemoine et Fils, in their catalog no. 149, along with 'La Perle'. Red-flowered.

'**Flamingo**' participated in the 1938 RHS Wisley Trials. No further information available.

'**Flamingo Lingo**' (Ware 1995) (*H. merriamii* × 'Silver Veil').
Compact, hard green buds give rise to profuse, early flowering. As the brownish pink stems unfurl, they hit a point, just before flowering, where they look like a sleeping flamingo. They continue to flower well into summer. Flowers are large for the size of plant and the 8- to 10-inch stems. Sun-proof and hardy to at least Zone 4. Performs well in a variety of soil types. Marketed as a seed strain by Alplains Seeds in 2000.

'**Florist's Choice**' (Terra Nova 2000).
This was selected from Terra Nova's field trials specifically for the specialty cut flower market, for its many tall, strong flowering stems. Flower spikes are nearly a yard tall in a rich red. The foliage makes a very nice mound. Plate 32.

'**Freedom**' AM 1938 (Blooms 1932).
Available as recently as 1993, this plant sports large rose-pink flowers that dangle from a compact 24-inch spray. Light green foliage. Strong sanguinea blood.

'**French Velvet**' (Terra Nova 1999, aka 'Velour Francais').
A hybrid of a pubescent form of *H. micrantha* and a silver-leaved form of a cross between *H. micrantha* and *H. americana*. Its large leaves are lightly patterned with silver and, most importantly, have the soft texture of velour. Bouquets of graceful creamy white flowers emerge in late spring. Persistently luxurious foliage. Plate 33.

'**Frosted Violet**' PPAF (Primrose Path 2003).
A vigorous plant sporting purple leaves with silvered patches that are subdued by the dark foliage. *Heuchera villosa* heritage. Tiny round rose-pink flowers, 30-inch flower spikes in May and June. Winter color is quite good with bluish violet accents. Quite drought-tolerant but will need sun protection.

'**Frühlicht**' (Light of Dawn).
This plant offers 16-inch spikes of red flowers over green foliage, blooming in June and July. We assume sanguinea heritage.

'Fusée' (Lemoine 1907).
A very distinctive 'Brizoides' cultivar that had ruby-red to partly dark maroon flowers held horizontally. "Brilliant yellow anthers" provided an exceptional contrast to the "somewhat somber flowers." No height or dimensions were listed.

'Gaiety' AM 1938 (Blooms 1932).
Taller than 'Freedom' at 30 inches. Carmine-red flowers are held erect.

'Geisha's Fan' (Terra Nova 2000) ('Veil of Passion' × crested seedling).
As the dark, veiled leaves mature, the leaves fan out, with more veins than normal, to a different leaf shape. Light pink flowers on stems 24 inches tall. Grow in shade to morning sun for best leaf color. Plate 34.

'Genevieve' (Lenz / Rancho Santa Ana Botanic Garden 1991) (*H. maxima* × *H. sanguinea*).
Glowing pink flowers have white centers, large upright flowers on 18-inch stems. The foliage is nicely marbled with gray. Flowers over a long period of time. Drought- and shade-tolerant. Hardy to Zone 8.

'Giant Scarlet' participated in the 1938 RHS Wisley Trials. No further information available.

'Gloire d'Orléans' (Lemoine) (NCCPG National Collection).
The collection obtained this sanguinea hybrid from Monique Chevry, Le Jardin d'Adoué, Lay-Saint-Christophe, France. Cream-colored flowers are on 16-inch flower spikes and bloom in May and June.

'Gloriana' (Blooms 1950, aka 'Captivation').
The flowers are a very deep pink. Available as recently as 1987; Blooms dropped this in favor of 'Carmen', which was thought to be superior.

'Gracillima' AM (Lemoine 1900).
This is a very old form, the first cross with *H. micrantha*, with many wiry sprays of small, soft pink flowers to 28 inches tall. The Lemoine et Fils Fall 1900 catalog states that the flowers resemble those of *Gypsophila paniculata* ("comme celles du *Gypsophila paniculata*"). Blooms in June. Some sources have this orig-

inating with Wallace in 1902, others with Arends in 1903. *Garden Chronicles* (31:298, 1902) has this as deriving from 'Brizoides', which Lemoine's correspondence confirms: this heuchera originated in Nancy, France, with Victor Lemoine, and involved 'Brizoides' with *H. micrantha*. Please refer to the 'Brizoides' listing for more details.

'Green Ivory' (Blooms 1968).
A selection of *H. cylindrica* 'Greenfinch'. May-blooming cylindrica hybrid with yard-tall spikes of cream blooms over green foliage.

'Green Light' (Wijnhout 2000).
Aart Wijnhout selected this cream-flowered form from an open-pollinated planting derived from Terra Nova varieties. Flower spikes are 16 inches tall. Foliage is green. Blooms in June and July.

'Green Spice' (Terra Nova 1993, aka 'Eco Improved').
The result of rigorous selection, it is more vigorous than its parent, *H. americana* 'Eco-magnififolia', and has much more color contrast. It still has Eco's dark gray-edged silver leaves with purple venation, but the leaves are smoother and a noticeably brighter green, as well as being somewhat larger. It has performed very well in New Zealand. Really great in the shade and looks exceptionally good in the fall with its zesty venation and color. This was renamed in New Zealand—the Kiwis (and many others) couldn't stand the original name, which sounded like an environmentally friendly detergent. Plate 35.

'Green Thumb'.
Diminutive type only 4 inches high with creamy white blossoms. A winner in the rock garden or as an edger, according to Lynn Ocone (personal communication to Dan Heims, 12 December 1994).

grossulariifolia 'Snowbells' (RHS Wisley List).
No further information available.

'Gypsy Dancer' (Terra Nova 2004).
This most floriferous hybrid, probably the most heavily blooming heuchera in existence, has a multitude of light pink flowers over low, dark, veiled foliage. A heavy repeat bloomer for part shade to full sun. Its compact habit keeps it looking tidy yet flashy. Does not require long cold treatments to

bloom. This is certainly one to try in warmer parts of California. Does well in darker locations. The plant is 12 inches wide and 8 inches tall, with flower spikes to 20 inches. A member of Terra Nova's Dance series. Plate 36.

'Harmonic Convergence' PP11111 (Primrose Path 1999).
This hybrid is truly a harmonic convergence of desirable traits in a heuchera: a combination of boldly patterned bronze and silver foliage and loose 18-inch spikes of frilly pink flowers produced over a long period in spring and early summer. Offered by Blooms of Bressingham.

'Hearts on Fire' PPAF (Primrose Path 2001).
This hybrid from Charles Oliver has ruffled leaves that are silver against a red background, marked with small patches of light gray. The flowers are white, and spikes are 24 inches tall. Won Best of Show at the 2001 North American Rock Garden Society show.

'Helen Dillon' (Dunlop).
This is a variegated sanguinea hybrid named by one of the world's greatest variegated plant collectors, Gary Dunlop, for Helen Dillon, designer and owner of one of the world's greatest small gardens. Propagated by Bob Brown. It has a mounding habit with cerise flowers on spikes to 18 inches tall. The variegation combines with silvering to nice effect.

'Hercules' EU 8174 (Oodshoorn 1999).
Another sanguinea hybrid with green and cream marbled foliage. It is similar to 'Monet' but larger. Twenty-inch spikes carry dark red flowers. Light shade. Blooms in May and June.

'High Society' (Terra Nova 1997) (*H. pubescens* × 'Pewter Veil').
This debutante, a lovely combination of sterling-silver foliage and large ivory flowers, did not have a very vigorous constitution, and so it has been quietly dropped from the Terra Nova line.

hirsutissima **'Santa Rosa'** (Kipping).
One of the most charming selections of this petite species collected by San Francisco plantsman Ted Kipping. Happiest in troughs or alpine houses, this plant needs special protection from overwatering. Propagated by tissue culture in the early 1990s. Twelve-inch spikes of pink and white tubular flowers

rise from petite rosettes only a few inches tall. Precious in the rock garden in a little crevice or in a trough. Plate 38.

'Hollywood' (Terra Nova 2005).
Dan feels this is one of the best and showiest heuchs to date—definitely in his Top 5! Strong reblooming spikes of dark coral flowers are produced over white-veiled, lightly ruffled metallic leaves. In flower all spring and summer. An amazing breakthrough in breeding. The plant is 9 inches tall and 12 inches wide, with 19-inch flower stalks. Plate 39.

'Huntsman' (Davidson 1951).
Originally called 'Dennis Davidson' by Beth Chatto as a way of acknowledging the breeder from Thropton, Northumberland. Bright salmon-pink flowers to 20 inches tall adorn this plant from late spring to midsummer; this red flower color precludes any notion that it is purely a selection from *H. cylindrica*. The foliage is unique: green marbled leaves with dark gray-brown venation.

'Hyperion' (Blooms 1959) (*H. cylindrica* × *H. sanguinea*).
Light pink blooms with a hint of green on very upright wands. Silvered foliage.

'Ibis' (Blooms 1950).
This deep pink sanguinea hybrid is a good long-blooming border plant. Does well in containers and in the rock garden, where it has proven to be quite drought-tolerant.

'Jack Frost' (Terra Nova 1995).
One of Terra Nova's earliest selections from a swarm of *H. sanguinea* crosses, the sole aim of which program was to select for the most brilliantly silvered and icy leaves. The flowers are bright red on 20-inch stalks with a beautifully compact mounding habit. As one might expect, this variety does well in containers and in the rock garden, where it has proven to be quite drought-tolerant, thanks to its U.S. Southwest heritage.

'Jade Gloss' (Primrose Path 2001).
This form has glossy, highly silvered leaves with bronze veining and large white flowers from pink buds in the spring. A heavy bloomer, with sturdy, erect flower stems to 18 inches.

'JEF's Splash' (Jolivot 2000).
A selection, possibly of *H. sanguinea* 'Snow Storm', made by Jean-Pierre Jolivot and named for his nursery, Les Jardins d'en Face. White-splashed leaves and red flowers.

'Jubilee' (Blooms 1935).
Named for King George V's Silver Jubilee in 1935. Clear pink flowers to 24 inches and compact foliage habit. This cultivar does well in containers and in the rock garden, where it has proven to be quite drought-tolerant.

'June Bride'.
The result of a sanguinea cross with the Bressingham Hybrids. Flowers are smaller but in higher density and numbers than straight *H. sanguinea* 'Alba', and their color is more of an ivory. This cultivar does well in containers and in the rock garden, where it has proven to be quite drought-tolerant.

'Just So' (Wijnhout 2000).
Aart Wijnhout selected this white-flowered form from an open-pollinated planting derived from Terra Nova varieties. Flower spikes are 18 inches tall. Foliage is green. Blooms in May.

'Key Lime Pie' (Terra Nova 2005).
This plant was chosen by Proven Winners to star in their Dolce series of plants, each with the name of a dessert. In the spring, the foliage with lightly ruffled edges is brilliant chartreuse as it emerges. Later in summer, the foliage is a more subdued chartreuse. Flower stalks are light coral with tiny white flowers. Plants are 7 inches tall and 16 inches wide, with 16-inch flower spikes. Plate 40.

'Kiki' (Detriché 2000).
Chance seedling that ascribes to a small, purple-leaved micrantha whose leaves go gray-green in winter. Bright, raspberry-red flowers. Not very vigorous, according to Jacques Detriché, but still very nice.

'Lace Ruffles' (Terra Nova 1994).
An early *H. americana* × *H. micrantha* hybrid with fleshy, silvered leaves with an undulating ruffle. Flowers were insignificant. 'Mint Frost' eventually supplanted this plant for its foliage color, and 'Can Can', another close relative, eclipsed it with its vivid leaves and superior ruffling.

129

'Lady in Red' (Witteman 2000).
This is a long-blooming form with 15-inch spikes of red flowers. Strong stems are good for cuts. Foliage is reddish purple; leaves are later muted with a silvered overlay.

Larenim Hybrids (Primrose Path 1989) (*H. pubescens* × red-flowered 'Brizoides').
These F_1 hybrids were retailed by Primrose Path in the early 1990s by mail order. Described in the Primrose Path catalog as having relatively large pink flowers on 18-inch stalks. Individuals were selected out and propagated as 'Larenim Queen' (see next entry) and 'Winter Red' (which also see).

'Larenim Queen' (Primrose Path 1997) (*H. pubescens* × red-flowered 'Brizoides').
This large and vigorous hybrid has green leaves with a hint of gray marbling and sprays of large pink flowers from 24 to 30 inches. Similar in size to earlier hybrids produced in Southern California ('Wendy', for example) but much hardier.

'Licorice' (Terra Nova 2005).
One of the darkest, shiniest, and largest seedlings to appear in our breeding program. Flowers are insignificant, but the huge, black leaves are a real draw. Spread can reach 3 feet in as many years, and the flower stalks are as high as 28 inches high by June. Adopted by Proven Winners, this plant will probably have a supporting role in their Black Magic & Purple Passion program. Plate 41.

'Lillian's Pink' (Rancho Santa Ana Botanic Garden 1990) (*H. maxima* × *H. sanguinea*).
A garden hybrid that occurred at Lillian Henningsen's garden in San Francisco, 'Lillian's Pink' is more medium-sized and compact than many of the large maxima hybrids. Pink flowers of a darker quality than most appear in dense inflorescences; stalks reach 18 to 24 inches over a tidy mound of medium-green leaves.

'Lime Rickey' (Terra Nova 2004).
This seedling of 'Amber Waves' is the first hybrid with ruffled lime foliage. It has small, attractive, pure white flowers and chartreuse leaves in the spring which turn to a lime-green in summer. Given minor protection, it is a vigor-

ous grower year-round. Eighteen inches wide and 8 inches tall, with 17-inch flower spikes. For shade only. Plate 42.

'Little Dark Girl' (Klinkhamer 1998).
An introduction from Dutch nurseryman Luc Klinkhamer derived from a seedling of Charles Oliver's 'Petite Pearl Fairy'. This plant sports small, dark brown leaves and carries pink flowers on 10-inch stalks.

'Magic Wand' AGM (Terra Nova 1997).
This strong-stemmed cultivar, a member of the Wand series, is derived from Slavic ('Pruhoniciana') and Western bloodlines. It is a great improvement over the muddy red-green flowers of 'Raspberry Regal', retaining the double-sized flowers, this time in a bright cerise, on 16-inch wand-shaped spikes. Plate 43.

'Mahogany' (NCCPG National Collection).
Bryan Russell, keeper of the collection, adds only that the foliage is oddly colored and that the plant is fairly vigorous in good soil.

'Mardi Gras' (Terra Nova 1998).
A variegated seedling from *H. americana* crosses. Typical americana dimensions and habit. Huge purplish-variegated leaves that range in color from coral to orange to green to gray. Flowers are not exciting, but the new foliage is delightful early in the year, either in the morning or late in the day, when it is backlit. Plate 44.

'Margarita' (Wijnhout 2000).
Aart Wijnhout selected this pink-flowered form from an open-pollinated planting derived from Terra Nova varieties. Flower spikes are 16 inches tall. Foliage is brown. Blooms from May to September.

'Marielle' (Wijnhout 2000).
Aart Wijnhout selected this pink-flowered form from an open-pollinated planting derived from Terra Nova varieties. Flower spikes are 27 inches tall. Foliage is green. Blooms from May to September.

'Marmalade' (Terra Nova 2004).
Related to 'Amber Waves', 'Marmalade' has rich, shiny, undulating foliage ranging in color from umber to deep sienna. Showy in all seasons, this plant

has heavy substance that stands up to inclement weather. Numerous, narrow spires of yellow-green flowers. Eighteen inches wide and 10 inches tall, with 16-inch flower spikes. Larger, less ruffled than 'Amber Waves', and more vigorous too, hence a good landscape choice. Plate 45.

'Mars' (Witteman 2002).
Evergreen purple-silver foliage patterned with dark veins. Insignificant flowers. Twelve-inch flower spikes bloom from May to July.

'Mary Rose' (Blooms 1932).
Available as recently as 1996, this old Blooms cultivar sported erect sprays of clear pink blooms to 20 inches. Participated in the 1938 RHS Wisley Trials.

'Mayfair' (Mayfair Nursery / Marcel LePiniec).
The result of a cross between 'Brizoides' and *H. hallii*, this plant is ideal for rock gardens and troughs and has light pink flowers over small tussocks of leaves.

'Mercury' (Witteman 2002).
Rounded, evergreen foliage with a blackish marbling pointing to *H. americana* breeding. Insignificant flowers on 22-inch flower spikes from May to July.

merriamii **'Primrose Path Selection'** (Primrose Path 1994).
Charles Oliver selected a particularly good individual of this small, mat-forming Klamath Range species, one with creamy white flowers, for propagation. It is a very pretty little plant with light green leaves.

micrantha **'Khaki Sheds'** (Brown).
"Ugly apricot sectoral variegations on brown leaves, open sprays of small nondescript coloured flowers," says Bob Brown of Cotswold Garden Flowers. Blooms in May and June, with spikes that are 21 inches tall.

micrantha **'Krinkles'** (Terra Nova 1994).
This seedling of *H. micrantha* 'Ridges' with extraordinarily sharp ruffling is still used as a breeding plant to introduce year-round very tight ruffling of the foliage. Flowers are like small white pearls on rather congested stalks to 18 inches (shorter than its forebears); the spread is nearly 2 feet. Foliage is apple-green with a white hairiness below. New spring growth is even more ruffled, with a few red tones along the edges. Blooms in June.

micrantha **'Martha Roderick'** (Smith 1983, aka 'Weott', 'Martha's
Compact').
Discovered and collected in the wild near Weott, California, off Highway 101
by Wayne Roderick and named for his mother. This is a splendid selection of
the species, with myriad feathery sprays of the lightest pink over a tight green
mound of foliage. Distributed by Nevin Smith of Suncrest Nurseries. Plate 46.

micrantha **'Painted Lady'** (Smith 1982).
A wild-collected form of *H. micrantha* with distinctive rugose (seersuckered)
silver-gray leaves with a purplish overlay. The white flowers are very tiny,
among the smallest in the genus, and are held on purple stems.

micrantha **'Ridges'** (Terra Nova 1990).
A seedling of *H. micrantha* 'Ruffles' showing very sharp ruffling as opposed to
the more rounded ruffles of *H. micrantha* 'Ruffles'. Dan used this plant in
breeding such hybrids as 'Purple Petticoats'. Flowers are small, rounded, and
white on hirsute stalks to 24 inches tall. Foliage is sharply rippled and apple-
green with a white hairiness below. New spring growth is even more ruffled.
The spread can exceed 2 feet. Blooms in early June.

micrantha **'Ruffles'** (Terra Nova 1991).
Originally from the garden of plantswoman Jane McGary. Dan picked up this
seedling in 1989, believing its intense ruffling would be helpful in breeding.
Flowers are small, rounded, and white on hirsute stalks to 22 inches tall.
Foliage is a flat apple-green with a white hairiness below. New spring growth
is extremely ruffled. The spread can exceed 2 feet. All ruffled heucheras, from
'Can Can' to 'Whirlwind', owe their form and style to this one exquisitely ruf-
fled plant, a one-in-a-million shot. Blooms in early June. Plate 47.

'Midnight Burgundy' (Primrose Path 2003) ('Regina' × 'Quilter's Joy').
This striking hybrid from Charles Oliver is an improved form of his 'Mid-
night Claret', more vigorous, larger, and more heavily veiled with light gray.
The flowers are creamy greenish, not showy but worth having.

'Midnight Claret' (Primrose Path 1999) ('Regina' × 'Quilter's Joy').
This hybrid from Charles Oliver has very dark purple leaves marked with
small patches of light gray. Being replaced by 'Midnight Burgundy' by Primrose Path.

Miniature Hybrids (Primrose Path 1992) (*H. pulchella* × *H. hallii*).
Marketed in the early 1990s by Primrose Path through mail order. They were
a series of plants with low mounds of small leaves and light pink flowers on
dark-colored 8- to 10-inch stems. Good drainage required, as with most rock
garden plants. Later called the San Pico Hybrids.

'Mini Mouse' (Wijnhout 1997).
Sixteen-inch spikes of whitish flowers arise over brown foliage.

'Mint Frost' (Terra Nova 1997).
A selected improvement of 'Emerald Veil'. Bright silver over a mint-green background with red petioles. Flowers are chartreuse and insignificant. Very shade-
tolerant and blooms well in the shade on 28-inch stalks. Plate 48.

'Molly Bush' AGM (Bush 1995).
Named after Allen Bush's daughter. 'Molly Bush' is a superior selection of *H.
villosa* f. *purpurea* 'Palace Purple' with broader leaves, a better, tighter habit,
and large, glossy, deep purple leaves, with more persistent purple coloration.
It holds up much better in the sun than does 'Palace Purple' and is very shade-
tolerant as well. The flowers are not distinctive and are on smaller stalks to
only 12 inches in height. Plate 49.

'Monet' (Terra Nova 1998).
Still among the best variegated heucheras, this plant's origin is shrouded in
mystery. Dan picked it up as a one-off at a Seattle flower show. Terra Nova's
plant has brilliant white foliage splashed with dark green; leaves turn pink in
the fall and are larger than most available variegated *H. sanguinea* selections.
Red flowers top off this vigorous selection. Good drainage necessary, as with
all sanguinea types. This name has also been seen in Europe attached to an
entirely different plant. Plate 50.

'Montrose Ruby' (Goodwin 1990) (*H. americana* 'Dale's Strain' × *H. villosa* f.
    purpurea 'Palace Purple').
A foundation plant and the seed parent of early crosses in the Primrose Path
and Terra Nova breeding programs. Early on, there was understandable vari-
ability in the intensity of the silvering and venation as well as the background
colors in this strain. Dan tells the story: "Of the original seven ['Montrose
Ruby' plants] that I bought from Nancy [Goodwin] at the then unheard-of

price of ten dollars apiece, I kept only three with superior coloration and venation and gave the others away. Unfortunately, one of these 'gifts' was then (unbeknownst to me) tissue-cultured by someone in large numbers. This is most likely the form seen in most gardens, based on the sheer numbers that were produced at the time. These poseurs are not nearly as attractive as the real thing." 'Montrose Ruby' can burn in full sun (as can both parents), so shade is recommended. Thanks go to Nancy Goodwin for this truly seminal plant, which has contributed so much to the evolution of hybrid heucheras.

'Moondrops' (Blooms) (*H. cylindrica* × *H. sanguinea*).
Lightly silvered leaves give rise to 18-inch spikes of cream-colored blooms kissed with pink.

'Mother of Pearl' (Chatto / RHS Wisley List) (NCCPG National Collection).
Pink flowers tinged with green on compact 18-inch spikes. Bold foliage is a dark green.

'Mt. St. Helens' (Sunny Border).
This is a typical strain of a hybrid *H. sanguinea* with red flowers to 20 inches over green foliage. Typical sanguinea care.

'Nancy' (Wijnhout 1997).
Aart Wijnhout himself selected this seedling from open-pollinated material. Twenty-four-inch flower spikes of beige-colored flowers in June. Foliage is brown.

'Neptune' (Witteman 2002).
Evergreen pewter-silver foliage with an undulating, dimensional habit. Insignificant flowers on 22-inch flower spikes from May to July.

'Northern Fire' (Marshall 1983) (*H. sanguinea* × *H. richardsonii*).
Considered the lesser of Marshall's three 1983 introductions, this floriferous heuch is still tough and tolerant of incredible cold. Sports rusty-red flowers on 18-inch spikes over green foliage. Bloom time is in June.

'Oakington Jewel' AM 1938 (Blooms 1932).
Alan and Dan were sitting together looking over an old Blooms catalog at Bloom's Norfolk home when Alan laughed to see the headline for this heu-

chera, trumpeting "Brand New for 1932!" More than seven decades later this plant (named for Bloom's old nursery) still intrigues, its silvered leaves, appliquéd purple, giving rise to pink-flowered spikes to 20 inches tall. Heuchera cognoscenti strongly suspect that Alan used an *H. americana* selection (similar to *H. americana* 'Eco-magnififolia') somewhere in the breeding. Originally and mistakenly attributed to Cultus Bay Nursery in Washington State; 'Cultus Bay Beauty' is the same plant as 'Oakington Jewel'.

'Oakington Superba' (Invalid Name).
Last listed in the *RHS Plant Finder* in 1990. RHS Wisley has no record of this plant.

'Obsidian' (Terra Nova 2002).
Black, really black, with broad, smooth, round leaves. Differs from 'Midnight Claret' and 'Midnight Burgundy' as its leaves are shiny with no veil. Sixteen inches wide and 10 inches tall, with 24-inch flower spikes. Flowers are small and chartreuse-white. Plate 51.

'Old La Rochette' (Victor Reiter / California Flora Nursery 1989) (*H. maxima* × *H. sanguinea*).
Creamy pink flowers are hairy on the outside and are held on stalks as long as 30 inches; they are urn-shaped, not as round as those of *H. maxima*. Leaves are pointed, with dentations that are more rounded but still less coarse than *H. maxima*, and about 1/3 the size. An impressive bloomer that makes a nice clump in time. Drought- and shade-tolerant. Like *H. maxima*, this hybrid makes a great groundcover for dry shade.

'Opal' (Lenz / Rancho Santa Ana Botanic Garden 1989) (*H. maxima* × *H. sanguinea*).
One of the largest white-flowered forms (buds are slightly pink), with large upright flowers on 2-foot stems. As with most RSABG hybrids, it is drought- and shade-tolerant. It would probably do well in some of the milder and sunnier sites in the United Kingdom.

'Orange Men' (Klinkhamer 1997).
This hybrid, derived from *H. americana* 'Dale's Strain', shows orange-green leaves that produce small cream flowers on 16-inch stalks. Its heritage dictates a shadier placement.

'Orphée' (Lemoine 1906, aka 'Orphei') (NCCPG National Collection).
First listed in the Lemoine et Fils catalog no. 164, which states that the flowers are a soft pink with a tinge of lilac on the tips. Listed by Blooms in 1951, it was later discovered in Germany by Joe Sharman and donated to the RHS Wisley Trials by German breeder Ernst Pagels.

'Palace Passion' (Terra Nova 1996).
The name for this hybrid, Terra Nova's first bronze-leaved heuchera with pink flowers, was inspired by all the hanky-panky that went on at Windsor Palace. The leaves are somewhat plain and leathery, and the pink flowers are on elegant stalks to 26 inches.

***parishii* 'Chiquita'** (Rancho Santa Ana Botanic Garden 1995).
Bart O'Brien has this to report, "'Chiquita' is a selection of *Heuchera parishii*, direct from the wild. It is a very dwarf form collected from White Knob in the San Bernardino Mountains by Tom Hayduk (RSABG staff) in 1991. It was named by Ramona Ferreira (also on the RSABG staff) . . . . It is very hardy, to at least Sunset zone 3 (and probably even Sunset zone 2) (USDA Zone 5)." Very low mats and flowers close to the foliage. Three-inch spikes support flowers with white petals and a pink calyx. Long summer bloom period.

'Patricia Louise'.
Another selection of 'Brizoides' that has been in use for years. Large pink bells on tall stems. Good cut flower with profuse blooming.

'Peach Flambé' (Terra Nova 2005).
Bright peach-colored leaves literally glow in spring and summer and turn to plum in winter. A vigorous medium-sized plant that produces white flowers in spring, it grows14 inches wide and 7 inches tall, with flower spikes to 16 inches. Wonderful as an accent or in a container. Plate 53.

'Peach Melba' (Terra Nova 2005).
This plant was chosen by Proven Winners to star in their Dolce series of plants, each with the name of a dessert. Unusual veiled leaves emerge a dark coral-peach in the spring and fade to a light peach in summer. Flower stalks rise to 24 inches tall with pink flowers. Foliar mounds are 7 inches tall and 18 inches wide. Plate 54.

'Peachy Keen' PPAF PVR (Terra Nova 2005).
Lovely large hot-pink flowers in cuttable spikes. Wildly splashed foliage in colors ranging from Day-Glo pink in spring to peach tones as it matures. A standout for variegatophiles—a splashed-leaf heuchera with pink and peach in the variegated areas! Ten inches tall and 12 inches wide, with 22-inch flower spikes. Plate 55.

'Peacock Feathers' (Terra Nova 1998).
A rare mutation of 'Plum Pudding' with small leaves shaped like peacock feathers. The plant has extremely heavy substance and a more rugose surface than 'Plum Pudding'. Color is darker and the leaves are barely 1 1/2 inches long on 3-inch petioles. Flowering is very rare. These dwarfs are only 4 inches tall and spread to 9 inches when mature. Plate 56.

'Pearl Drops' (Blooms 1950).
A delicate introduction with an arching 24-inch inflorescence of white flowers, just kissed with pink.

'Pearl Pendants' (Primrose Path 2000, aka 'Pearl Drops', which name was taken by Blooms a half century earlier, see previous entry).
This hybrid from Charles Oliver has large, teardrop-shaped pale pink flowers on 24-inch stems. They spring from light bronze foliage that has just a titch of silver marking.

'Persian Carpet' (Terra Nova 1995) ('Ruby Veil' × 'Pewter Veil').
This genetic combo of two members of the Veil series yielded a wild potpourri of interwoven shades of purple, silver, and gray. The colors change with the seasons. Considered by many to be one of Terra Nova's best for European gardens and very popular in England. Insignificant flowers. Plate 57.

'Petite Bronze Pearl' (Primrose Path 1997).
This member of the Petite series has leaves of solid bronze and light pink flowers on 15-inch stalks.

'Petite Lime Sherbet' (Primrose Path 1997).
This hybrid's small green leaves are boldly marked with silver veining, and the bright pink flowers are carried on stalks to 12 inches.

'Petite Marbled Burgundy' PP11059 (Primrose Path 1997).
Bronzy red leaves with strong silver markings, light pinkish white flowers on 12-inch stalks.

'Petite Pearl Fairy' PP11058 (Primrose Path 1997).
When Dan visited Charles Oliver and saw all the Petites sitting in a row, he admired this hybrid most, with its small bronze leaves marbled with silver and medium-pink flowers on 10-inch stalks. Notes from the RHS Wisley Trials for rock garden heucheras were concise: "Best foliage!" Plate 58.

'Petite Pink Bouquet' (Primrose Path 1997).
Leaves are green with light silver misting, large medium-pink flowers on 12-inch stalks.

'Petite Ruby Frills' (Primrose Path 1999).
Bronze leaves with silver markings, pink-flowered stalks to 12 inches. This form makes a clump intermediate in size between 'Petite Pearl Fairy' and 'Petite Marbled Burgundy'.

Petite series (Primrose Path 1997).
Several western montane species and 'Brizoides' selections were hybridized to create these compact, rock or woodland garden plants. They keep their best coloration and habit in lean, gritty soil. All are stunning in the garden en masse and do best in full sun.

'Pewter Moon' (Oudolf 1992).
Introduced by Dutch designer and breeder Piet Oudolf. Leaves are marbled and give rise to short spikes of light pink flowers in May. Named by Rod Richards of Richalps Nursery, Hampshire, United Kingdom. Plate 59.

'Pewter Veil' (Terra Nova 1992).
Terra Nova's first patented plant, the result of *H. americana* backcrossed to selected forms of 'Montrose Ruby', which was then considered a strain. The large and lovely pewter-embossed leaves have a pearly pink finish in spring. The flowers are green with purple, and the spikes are quite tall (30 inches). Perfect in containers and more shade-tolerant than many. Plate 60.

Pike's Peak Hybrids (Primrose Path 1992).
A hybrid series, the result of a cross between the Colorado alpine species *H. hallii* and a bright red clone of 'Brizoides'. Pink flowers on 12-inch stems.

'Pink Charmer' (Wijnhout 1997).
Twelve-inch spikes of pink flowers over green leaves. Blooms in May.

'Pink Delight' AM 1925, AM 1938 (Blooms 1938).
Participated in the 1938 RHS Wisley Trials. Bloom's 1951 catalog says it is the same as 'Apple Blossom', which see for more info.

'Pink Lipstick' (Terra Nova 2004).
Lipstick-shaped columnar spikes of pink flowers are quite distinctive. The foliage is green, vigorous, and low-growing. Evergreen with nice red overtones on the winter foliage. Fourteen inches wide and 7 inches tall, with 24-inch flower spikes.

'Pink Love' (Wijnhout 1997) (Jelitto seedling).
Silver leaves with pink flowers on 24- to 28-inch stalks. Blooms in May.

'Pink Ruffles' (Terra Nova 1993).
An early hybrid with ruffled foliage and pink flowers. In 1995, in a skit entitled "The Customer" staged by the Perennial Plant Association in Minneapolis, Minnesota, Dan played the role of 'Pink Ruffles', flanked by two actors who were his "companion plants." The production closed gracefully after one performance. Dan complained to his agent that "it" (playing a plant—especially a heuchera) wasn't enough of a "stretch."

'Pink Spray' (Blooms 1924).
An early cross of 'Gracillima' and *H. sanguinea* 'Trevor Red'. Lost in the disruption of the war years, it was rediscovered by Mary Ramsdale in 1988. A brighter pink than 'Gracillima'.

'Pink Wave' (Emery / Santa Barbara Botanic Garden 1991) (F_2 sanguinea hybrid × *H. elegans*).
Dense mats 9 to 18 inches across composed of many rosettes of rich, medium-green semi-glossy leaves. Compound racemes of many small, rose-

pink, bell-shaped flowers. Flowers in midspring. Takes full sun in maritime sites with adequate moisture but inland prefers afternoon shade. Hardy to Zone 6.

'Pluie de Feu' (Rain of Fire) (Lemoine 1902, aka 'Feurregen').
A 'Brizoides' hybrid that Lemoine judged very superior to *H. sanguinea* for its vigor and the number of flowers. The original cultivar was described as having flowers the color of "carmine-strawberry." Stems to 20 inches.

'Plum Pudding' (Terra Nova 1996).
With heritage in 'Ruby Veil' and 'Can Can', this plant (sometimes seen listed with the "g" dropped) really is one of the best of the best and easily makes it into Dan's Top 5 list of heucheras. Collector's Nursery's 1999 catalog effuses, "This one literally outshines the rest with leaves of shimmery plum purple [and] a tight growth habit. . . . Our most popular." Looks very good early in the season in northern climates and makes an excellent foil for variegated silver and gold plants. The flowers are insignificant but in no way detract from the beauty of the plant. Plate 61.

'Pretty Polly' (Blooms 1950).
A darling at only 12 inches tall, it is certainly one of the freest bloomers, making a prodigious production of petite rose-pink posies.

'Prince' (Wijnhout 1997).
Dark purple, palmate leaves are heavily ruffled. Flower stalks are purple and carry small white flowers on 20-inch spikes in May.

'Prince of Silver' (Wijnhout 2002).
Evergreen silver foliage with pale cream flowers. Twenty-two-inch flower spikes in June and July. Said to be a fast grower. Derived from Terra Nova stock. Patented by Witteman, B.V.

'Profusion' (Lemoine 1904).
A sensational 'Gracillima' selection (the Lemoine catalog declared it the equal of 'Gracillima') which produced a wealth of graceful, tubular ivory-white flowers on stems over a yard long! It also had nicely dentate leaves. Named for its prolific production of flowers. Quite a plant.

'Pruhoniciana' (aka 'Pruhonica', Dr. Sitar's Hybrids).
A seed strain of hybrids of *H. cylindrica* and *H. sanguinea* containing flowers of pink, pale red, light brown, and, unfortunately, an inordinate amount of ugly green. They are held on extremely strong spikes to 36 inches tall. Kees Sahin, a Dutch seedsman, worked with Sitar in the Czech Republic to introduce this strain of heucheras. Pruhonice is a lovely village on the southeast outskirts of Prague and home of the Academy of Sciences and the Institute of Botany, where Sitar worked.

pubescens **'Hob'.**
Says Bob Brown of Cotswold Garden Flowers, "The winter leaves are a dull glowing orange-red and look wonderful with orange primroses, white flowers." This undemanding plant blooms in May and June; spikes are 18 inches tall.

'Purple Mountain Majesty' PPAF (Primrose Path 2004).
One of Charles Oliver's favorite introductions with tight purple foliage that is lightly silvered. The white flowers that emerge from the 24-inch stalks are larger than their earlier introductions. Plants are 10 inches high and18 inches across. Very sun-tolerant according to Oliver. Plate 63.

'Purple Petticoats' AGM (Terra Nova 1997) ('Chocolate Ruffles' × 'Ruby Ruffles').
Frilly, dark purple foliage adorns this tough beauty. 'Purple Petticoats' placed first for winter foliage at a top European horticultural show during one of Holland's toughest winters. "Excellent winter presence," according to the 1999 Heronswood Nursery catalog. Unique texture and, you guessed it, insignificant flowers. Plate 64.

'Purple Sails' (Terra Nova 1997).
From the *H. micrantha* × *H. americana* trials came this most wonderful lavender-purple individual with maple-shaped leaves, undulating, upright, and with a metallic finish. Four-inch leaves can spiral into an amazing helix when the plant is happy and mature. Plate 65.

'Quilter's Joy' AGM (Primrose Path 1997) ('Montrose Ruby' × 'White Marble').
Crisply defined silver markings on a bronze background give this selection its patchwork look. White flowers on 18- to 24-inch stems in late spring. Winter hardy to at least Zone 4. 'Quilter's Joy' was inadvertently and briefly distrib-

uted as 'Checkers' when that one label somehow got misplaced in transit to the Terra Nova stockhouse. The confusion was cleared up through trials in Holland, which showed these plants are, indeed, one and the same; therefore, all 'Checkers' shall become 'Quilter's Joy'. Terra Nova apologizes to the industry and The Primrose Path.

'Rachel' (Ramsdale 1990) (*H. villosa* f. *purpurea* 'Palace Purple' × 'Sunset').
Named for Mary Ramsdale's granddaughter, who is pictured in the plate with her namesake plant. Flowers are rose-pink and smaller than *H. sanguinea*, one of the parents of 'Sunset'. 'Rachel' does better in the maritime Northwest with full sun. Foliage is purple, although lighter, smoother, and smaller than 'Palace Purple'. The sister seedling to 'Rachel' is 'David', which see. Plate 66.

'Rakete' (Rocket) (Frikart 1935).
A German introduction. Flower spikes of dark vermilion-red rise over 2 feet tall from early to late summer.

'Raspberry Ice' PP13340 (Primrose Path 2003).
Dark, burgundy-purple foliage highlighted by silvered patches stained rose. Rose-pink flowers are held on 24-inch spikes in May and June. Can become quite large when well grown: Charles Oliver reports plants 2 feet wide in as many years. Carried by Blooms.

'Raspberry Regal' AGM (Englerth 1985).
An early 'Pruhoniciana' introduction by Larry Englerth and a more widely distributed member of the 'Pruhoniciana' club, with very strong, nearly yard-high stems of undistinguished greeny red. The flower, though, will improve in full sun. The rosette is neat and 9 inches tall.

'Red Arrow' (Laurens Lageschaar 1995).
This Dutch introduction, a seedling from Heinz Klose's 'Feuerlohe', carries green leaves and red flowers atop spikes to 16 inches tall.

'Red Bird' (Wijnhout 1997).
Sixteen-inch spikes of cream flowers over brown leaves. Blooms in June.

'Red Pimpernel' (1932).
Available in the Blooms catalog in the 1930s, where this sanguinea hybrid

was listed as having "flowers of bright crimson-red." A very vigorous habit. Blooms to 24 inches. This cultivar does well in containers and in the rock garden, where it has proven to be quite drought-tolerant.

'Red Spangles' AGM (Blooms 1950).
Considered by Alan Bloom to be "the ultimate blood-red." Long-lasting flowers on stems to 20 inches tall arise from a dense, full rosette of foliage. Participated in the 1954 RHS Wisley Trials.

'Regal Robe' (Terra Nova 1997) ('Ruby Veil' × 'Emerald Veil').
Among the better heucheras Dan has seen out of Terra Nova's breeding program and a personal favorite of his. Fascinating silver-lavender marbled leaves to 10 inches across, yet the plant is compact. The leaves are decidedly maple-shaped and metallic. Plate 67.

'Regina' AGM (Primrose Path 1997) ('Quilter's Joy' × 'Chatterbox').
This hybrid must be one of the most beautiful, tall purple-leaved, pink-flowered heucheras in existence. It has silvered, burgundy-bronze leaves and light pink flowers on 36-inch stems in late spring to early summer. The stunning foliage makes it a major conversation stop in people's gardens. In September 1997, 'Regina' won a first prize at the Royal Society for Horticulture Perennial Plant Exposition in Lisse, The Netherlands.

'Rhapsody' AM 1963 (Blooms 1963).
Considered among the best pink-flowered forms in the 1960s, this cultivar does well in containers and in the rock garden, where it has proven to be quite drought-tolerant. Twenty-four-inch spikes.

'Rickard' (NCCPG National Collection).
No information from the collection holder.

'Ring of Fire' (Terra Nova 1995).
This hybrid selection of *H. americana* 'Eco-magnififolia' is an exquisite silver-leaved plant suffused with purple along the veins. Colors change with the seasons; the excitement comes in fall, when—if nights are cold enough—the leaves develop an edge of bright coral (hence the name). Small green flowers, just like *H. americana* 'Eco-magnififolia'. Plate 68.

'Rondi' (Wijnhout 1997).
Sixteen-inch spikes of cream flowers over green leaves. Blooms in May.

'Ronstar' (Wijnhout 1997).
Sixteen-inch spikes of pink flowers over brown leaves. Blooms in May.

'Rosada' (Davis Arboretum 1991) (*H. maxima* × *H. sanguinea*).
Known at the Davis Arboretum for years simply as T796, this hybrid, which grew in the Foothill section from collections made between 1941 and 1958, is now known to be the result of a cross made by Don Sexton, former superintendent of the arboretum. Very similar in bloom to 'Old La Rochette' but with creamy pink flowers, which are prolifically produced under the long, hot California summer on 24- to 36-inch stems. The plant's leaves are dark green and round to oval in outline without coarse dentations. A planting in a sunny location on the Davis campus has survived and thrived to become a tough arboretum favorite. Also does well in dappled shade. Hardy to Zone 8.

'Rosamonde' AM 1903 (Arends 1903, aka 'Rosamunde', 'Rosamundi')
    (NCCPG National Collection).
Distributed and sold by Blooms in 1933, this superior hybrid of 'Gracillima' and *H. micrantha* 'Rosea' (also an AM winner) was an early George Arends introduction. Terra-cotta flowers are carried on large arching sprays to 36 inches tall.

'Rosea Perfecta' participated in the 1938 RHS Wisley Trials. No further information available.

'Rosemary Bloom' PP10441 (Blooms 1999, aka 'Heuros').
This Blooms introduction was named for the wife of Adrian Bloom, Alan's son. Flowers are coral-pink, and the foliage has strong substance. Spikes are between 18 and 24 inches tall. It is a strong rebloomer, according to the Blooms of Bressingham Web site.

'Rose Mirrors' PP13140 (Primrose Path 2003).
Dark, rounded purple foliage highlighted by silvered patches stained rose. Rose-pink flowers, 18-inch flower spikes in May and June. This is one of Primrose Path's darkest-leaved plants.

'Rosenrot' (Rose-red) (NCCPG National Collection).
A German introduction. No further information available.

'Royal Velvet' PPAF (Primrose Path 2004).
This Oliver introduction has pubescent leaves of rich purple with silver high-lights. Eighteen-inch flower stalks bloom in spring, much sooner than do those of *H. villosa*, and the white flowers are much more attractive to boot.

'Ruberrima' is mentioned in Trehane's *Index Hortensis*. No further information available.

rubescens **'Troy Boy'.**
Selection made by Roy Davidson from Troy Peak, Nye County, Nevada, in 1973. First distributed by Grand Ridge Nurseries in Washington and later sold by Rice Creek Gardens in Minnesota. Appropriate for the trough or a well-positioned crevice in a rock garden, this little gem will throw 4-inch spikes of moderately pink flowers from mat-like rosettes a mere inch or two high. To quote Davidson (*Rock Garden Quarterly* vol. 50, no. 2), "'Troy Boy' is . . . the tiniest and tidiest of alum-roots." Quite possibly the smallest heuchera in cultivation and one that every rock gardener wants.

'Rubis' (Lemoine 1904).
A noteworthy 'Brizoides' hybrid in that Lemoine claimed it had the largest flowers of any in the genus. The flowers were carmine-magenta with a ruby nuance. As if this wasn't enough, the beautiful foliage was a marbled dark and clear green, and it had strong stems that rose up 30 inches.

'Ruby Mist' COPF (Morden / Collicutt 1985) (*H. sanguinea × H. richardsonii*).
Selected from a population of open-pollinated seedlings of no. 64-1, which in turn, is an open-pollinated seedling population of 'Brandon Pink'. More consistently floriferous than 'Northern Fire', which is a sibling of 'Brandon Pink' and 'Brandon Glow'. 'Ruby Mist' is generally considered to be an improvement over 'Brandon Pink'. Compact plants 8 to 10 inches wide and 3 to 4 inches high give rise to 20- to 24-inch stalks with red flowers of varying intensity.

'Ruby Ruffles' (Terra Nova 1995).
Another early Terra Nova introduction that had limited distribution. 'Ruby

Ruffles' was kin to 'Chocolate Ruffles' but with color more in the ruby tones. With continued trialing and selection, this cultivar was dropped in favor of other forms. Flowers are not very distinctive.

'Ruby Veil' (Terra Nova 1991).
'Ruby Veil' has incredible leaves up to 8 inches across with metallic slate-gray venation over velvety ruby-red foliage. This is one of the earliest crosses using 'Montrose Ruby' and select seedlings of *H. americana* 'Dale's Strain'. It is very sun-tolerant and reliable. Flowers are small and white on immense purple scapes. Plate 70.

'Sanbrot' (NCCPG National Collection).
No information from the collection holder.

'Sancyl' (Wolley-Dod 1902) (*H. sanguinea* × *H. cylindrica*).
Charles Wolley-Dod had an article in *The Garden* (4 October 1902) in which he, as the breeder, proposed this cultivar's name, an amalgam of "sanguinea" and "cylindrica"; thus, 'Sancyl'—if it *is* the same plant—would take precedence over 'Edge Hall' and 'Edge Hybrid' (a name that Wolley-Dod himself used when he first distributed this plant), which names would then be superseded and therefore invalid. See 'Edge Hall' for more info.

'Sanglant' (Lemoine 1905).
A 'Brizoides' selection first listed in the Lemoine et Fils catalog no. 161. A significant cultivar in that it was the first silver-marbled leaf selection to be offered in horticulture. The flowers were described as being "enormous, clear blood-red and the most brilliant of all heucheras." The cost then was just five francs.

sanguinea **'Alba'** AGM.
First mentioned in *Gartenflora* in 1896 and ascribed as a species to German nurserymen Haage and Schmidt. This white-flowered sport of the normally cerise *H. sanguinea* has flower spikes that are 16 inches tall over green foliage.

sanguinea **'Cherry Splash'** (Terra Nova 1994).
Another early Terra Nova introduction from the time when the Veil and Splash series were introduced. Its companions were *H. sanguinea* 'Coral Splash' and *H. sanguinea* 'Splish Splash'; Dan selected all three. Flowers are cherry-red and contrast highly with the foliage.

sanguinea **'Coral Splash'** (Terra Nova 1994).
An early variegated Terra Nova introduction selected when the Veil and Splash series were introduced. Not too vigorous, it is now virtually absent from horticulture. Flowers are light coral on 16-inch spikes. Foliage is variegated but subtler than *H. sanguinea* 'Cherry Splash' or *H. sanguinea* 'Splish Splash'.

sanguinea **'Crimson Cloud'** (Smith).
A dark red sanguinea selection sold by Suncrest Nurseries. Selected as a standout from a large planting of *H. sanguinea* 'Leuchtkäfer'. Said to be one of the darkest reds in cultivation, this variety does well in containers and in the rock garden, where it has proven to be quite drought-tolerant.

sanguinea **'Fackel'** (Torch).
A good German seed strain of dark scarlet bells on 16-inch stalks. It has the typical sanguinea foliage and shape. Good cut flower.

sanguinea **'Frosty'** (Terra Nova 1995).
This straight selection of a species has brilliant coral-pink flowers along with unique frosted and variegated foliage. Good drainage is necessary. Does well in containers and in the rock garden, where it has proven to be quite drought-tolerant. Plate 73.

sanguinea **'Gold Dust'** (Terra Nova 1998).
A rare selection from the Terra Nova field trials which is delightfully flecked with golden yellow. Gold variegation is quite rare in *Heuchera*. Flower spikes are 16 inches tall with light cerise flowers. Plate 74.

sanguinea **'Hailstorm'** (Dunlop 1996).
A brightly variegated selection and a very fine one at that! Joe Sharman, a co-owner of Monksilver Nursery, has a beautiful specimen with brilliant red flowers in his garden in Cambridge, England. It would appear to have *H. sanguinea* 'Snow Storm' in its pedigree and has much to offer variegatophiles. Plate 75.

sanguinea **'Leuchtkäfer'** (Firefly) (aka 'Glow Worm').
A most popular seed strain in the United States, having slightly hairy leaves and very dark red flowers on 24-inch spikes. It has been a source of much selection and hybridizing. The flowers are fragrant. This cultivar does well in containers and in the rock garden, where it has proven to be quite drought-

tolerant. It combines well with ornamental grasses, salvias, evening prim-roses, and nepetas, and helps cool the roots and cover the ugly stems of roses.

sanguinea **'Maxima'** (Invalid Name).
First mentioned in 1905 and included in *The RHS Dictionary of Gardening* as recently as 1991, where this selection is described as having burgundy flowers.

sanguinea **'Miss Jessop'** is found in Perry's Hardy Plant Farm's 1931 cata-log, which describes it as a "very pretty free flowering variety with dainty spikes of rose-crimson flowers."

sanguinea **'Nancy Perry'** AM 1911 (Perry 1911).
Listed in Perry's Hardy Plant Farm's 1911 catalog. This plant has 30-inch spikes of bright rose-pink flowers, profusely produced.

sanguinea **'Petworth'** AM 1938 (Wells 1934).
The 8-inch mound of medium-green foliage gives rise to 24-inch spikes of scarlet flowers. It was placed in trial in 1934 as an improved form of *H. san-guinea* having clear color and "freedom of blossom." Considered "brightest variety" in 1934 and a winner at the 1938 RHS Wisley Trials; a full description appeared in the *Journal of the RHS* (1938) 63:543.

sanguinea **'Red Eric'** (Charles Bloom 1934).
A rosy scarlet selection of the species with very large blooms over 6-inch mounds of dark green foliage. Flower spikes are 24 inches tall. Said to be quite free-flowering. Participated in the 1938 RHS Wisley Trials.

sanguinea **'Ruby Bells'** (Benary Seed 2004).
Profuse dark red flowers are carried over dark evergreen foliage. The breeders claim a light fragrance, which we have yet to experience. The foliage mound is 6 inches tall and 12 inches wide, with 16-inch spikes of flowers. This June-bloomer is from Ernst Benary of Muenden, Germany.

sanguinea **'Sioux Falls'.**
Eighteen-inch spikes of rich red flowers in June. Foliage is light green with some silver overlay. Sold as a seed strain in the United States but marketed as a cultivar by Beeches Nursery in England.

sanguinea **'Snow Storm'** (Terra Nova 1989).
Brilliantly variegated foliage, splashed white with a darker green edge. The cerise-red flowers provide a wonderful contrast. Requires good drainage. This was the plant that built Terra Nova (see chapter 4); before its introduction it was trialed at Boskoop in The Netherlands against *H. sanguinea* 'Taff's Joy' and a variegated form of *H. sanguinea* 'Leuchtkäfer'. *Heuchera sanguinea* 'Snow Storm' showed the most vigor of the three. (Dan would now choose 'Snow Angel' or 'Monet' for even better vigor.) Plate 76.

sanguinea **'Splendens'.**
Mentioned in early twentieth-century literature (*Rev. Hort. Belg.* 32:208, 1906) and an accepted name in the RHS Horticultural Database, this form (sold as a seed strain or as vegetatively propagated plants) has been a standby in the garden for dependable, clear red flowers and tight evergreen foliage. Very drought-resistant, this plant has a great following in the U.S. Desert Southwest and is well established in French horticultural circles. Height is 20 inches, and the plant has a 12-inch spread. Blooms from late spring into early summer.

sanguinea **'Splish Splash'** (Terra Nova 1996).
Wonderfully splashed foliage with more green than *H. sanguinea* 'Snow Storm'. The foliage takes on a fabulous pink flush in winter, and red-pink flowers brighten the plant in late spring. Requires good drainage. This was another in the Splash series, which included *H. sanguinea* 'Cherry Splash' and *H. sanguinea* 'Coral Splash'—all variegated forms; Bill Janssen of Collector's Nursery named this one, which made the biggest splash of the Splashes. It has also proven quite hardy: its good performance is reported in Calgary, Alberta (Zone 2).

sanguinea **'Taff's Joy'** (Taffler).
A red and cream variegated seedling from Stephen Taffler, master of the English language and guru of all things variegated. Lovely pink flowers and pink winter color.

sanguinea **'Walker's Variety'.**
Seen listed thus in the French horticulture compendium "Collections de Pleine Terre" of 1909 (and in the RHS Horticultural Database currently), this old turn-of-the-century plant may instead be a 'Brizoides' hybrid. It has open spikes of rose flowers. Leaves are well silvered. Does well in containers and in

the rock garden, where it has proven to be quite drought-tolerant. Spikes are 20 to 24 inches tall.

sanguinea 'White Cloud' (Suncrest Nurseries 1985).
An albino selection with creamy white flowers on 16-inch spikes. A seed strain from the mid 1980s, it is still carried by Jelitto Seed of Germany but is rare in North American horticulture.

sanguinea 'White Empress'.
This one was found in Perry's Hardy Plant Farm 1931 catalog, where the selection is billed as "a decided improvement over the old *H. alba*." Obviously, it has clear white flowers.

'San Pico Rosita' (Primrose Path 1996) (*H. hallii* × *H. pulchella*).
The precursor of 'San Pico Rosita' was what Oliver at first called the Miniature Hybrids (see earlier listing). He finally selected and propagated the best and named it 'San Pico Rosita'. This name derived from the sites of the parent species, San Juan Mountains (New Mexico) for *H. pulchella* and Pike's Peak (Colorado) for *H. hallii*; "rosita" is a diminutive meaning "little rosey" (the small flowers are rosy to light pink in color). The small green leaves are characteristic of the parents. It is an early bloomer (in May), like many western, montane species.

'Santa Ana Cardinal' (Lenz / Rancho Santa Ana Botanic Garden 1991) (*H. maxima* × *H. sanguinea*).
This plant is a dramatic staple of the Southern California landscape. Up to 3 feet tall in flower, it sports spikes of rose-red, bell-shaped calyces with tiny pink petals set on a maroon-colored rachis. The leaves are rounded, with scalloped margins that indicate the sanguinea heritage. Drought- and shade-tolerant.

'Santa Cruz' (Monksilver / RHS Wisley List).
Joe Sharman of Monksilver Nursery calls this plant "a wilding which may be a form of *H. glabra* or *H. micrantha*."

'Sashay' (Terra Nova 1998).
This plant was a surprise mutation of 'Purple Petticoats'. The upper leaf layer is green (not purple as in 'Purple Petticoats'), which gives a fascinating two-tone leaf. Very tough and cold-resistant like its original form, 'Purple Petti-

coats'. The flower spikes are 16 inches tall; flowers are acceptable but not showy. Plate 78.

'Saturn' (Witteman 2002).
Evergreen rounded silver-green foliage with dark veins. Edges are narrowly painted with red. Insignificant flowers. Twenty-two-inch flower spikes from May to July.

'Saturnale' (Lemoine 1907).
A 'Brizoides' selection that made its way into the 1938 RHS Wisley Trials courtesy of Belgian horticulturist Van Egmond. Twenty-inch spikes carry dull scarlet flowers with maroon tips over very dark green leaves in 6-inch mounds. Blooms in May and June. Generally thought to be lost to cultivation, as are most of Lemoine's Brizoides Group.

'Schneewittchen' (Snow White) (aka 'Schneeweissen').
A German introduction. Its leaves are lightly variegated, and the plant carries white flowers 18 to 22 inches above the foliage. Better in part shade.

'Scintillation' HC 1956, AM 1957, AGM 1993 (Blooms 1950).
Considered by many to be a hybrid with a lot of sanguinea genes. This "firm favorite" was further described in *Alan Bloom's Hardy Perennials* (1991) as having "coral rimmed, deep pink bells on 24" stems." Leaves are well marbled as well. This cultivar does well in containers and in the rock garden, where it has proven to be quite drought-tolerant.

'Shady Barbara' (Brown 1998).
Discovered by Barbara Langston of Cotswold Garden Flowers, the catalog of which describes it thus: "Nice evergreen pale green feathery pinwheel leaves and red flowers." Blooms on 16-inch spikes in May and June.

'Shamrock' (Terra Nova 2000).
Great flowers of shamrock-green tower 36 inches above the rosette. This is a superior, long-lasting cut flower. The foliage has a subtle silvery overlay. Takes a place near the redoubtable *H. cylindrica* 'Greenfinch' as another excellent (if somewhat brighter) green flower. Plate 79.

'Shenandoah Mountain' PPAF (Primrose Path 1999).
Vigorous and large, this Primrose Path introduction sports bronze foliage with dark veining. Flower stems have leafy bracts and rise to 30 inches in late spring. Flowers are smallish and creamy white. This plant prefers light shade.

'Shere Variety'.
Available in the Blooms catalog (but not their introduction) from 1932 through 1939, this product of *H. sanguinea* and 'Brizoides' was listed as "very attractive and free-flowering, producing short spikes of bright scarlet flowers over most of the summer." Spikes are 18 inches tall. Like many of its type, this cultivar does well in containers and in the rock garden, where it has proven to be quite drought-tolerant. Participated in the 1938 and 1954 RHS Wisley Trials.

'Silberreggen' (Silver Rain) (Junge 1935).
This sanguinea type from Germany has pure white flowers to 20 inches tall. It remains one of the best white-flowered sanguineas. This cultivar does well in containers and in the rock garden, where it has proven to be quite drought-tolerant.

'Silky' (Wijnhout 1997).
Twenty-inch spikes of cream flowers over green leaves. Blooms in May.

'Silver Indiana' EBR (van den Top 1999).
This cultivar by Dutch nurseryman Jan van den Top, of Barneveld, The Netherlands, is presumably the result of crosses of *H. americana* hybrids. Its silver-marbled leaves and flower spikes to 14 inches with white flowers have been enthusiastically greeted. Plate 80.

'Silver Light' PPAF (Primrose Path 2003).
Deeply lobed foliage is highly metallic and will brighten dark corners of the garden. Eighteen-inch flowers are a "frilly, light pink" and bloom in late spring.

'Silver Lode' PP13339 (Primrose Path 2001).
Rounded and lobed foliage has a pewter patina with a burgundy reverse. Late spring brings 36-inch flower spikes carrying small white flowers.

'Silver Maps' (Primrose Path 2000).
This is a sibling of 'Silver Scrolls' but has smaller leaves with extensive silver markings on a bronze background. It has a compact habit with looser wands of white flowers on 18-to 20-inch stems in spring.

'Silver Mittens' (2004).
A silver-speckled heuchera with mitten-shaped leaves. Red flowers in May and June. Listed in Dutchman Luc Klinkhamer's Perennial Page and in Bob Brown's Cotswold Garden Flowers. No other word on its origin.

'Silvero' (Wijnhout 1997).
Six-inch spikes of pink flowers over silver leaves. Blooms in May.

'Silver Scrolls' PP12066 (Primrose Path 1999) ('Harmonic Convergence' × 'Petite Bronze Pearl').
The rounded leaves are metallic silver marked with scrollwork of dark veining. The leaves are so reflective that good clumps will considerably brighten shadier parts of the garden. The foliage is very weather-resistant and tough, looking attractive even after a hard winter. It has showy wands of white flowers tinged with pink in spring to 24 inches. Won a Bronze Medal at Plantarium 2000 in Holland. One of Oliver's best! Plate 81.

'Silver Shadows' (Terra Nova 1997) ('Pewter Veil' × 'Regal Robe').
In spring, this has pure, shimmering dark silver leaves with a rose overlay. Excellent habit with thick 7-inch leaves. Since its picture first appeared in the November 1995 issue of *Fine Gardening* magazine, it has become a most sought-after plant. Terra Nova meant it to be an improvement or substitute for 'Pewter Veil', as it had a neater habit with shorter petioles; but because people knew 'Pewter Veil' and loved it, Terra Nova continued to support 'Pewter Veil' as well. The flowers are not showy on either. Plate 82.

'Silver Veil' (Terra Nova 1992).
Among the earliest Terra Nova introductions and a charter member of the Veil series, with genetic makeup much more on the sanguinea side. It has showy 20-inch stalks with cerise flowers and very strong silvering and veining on the leaves.

'Silvo' (Wijnhout 1997).
Six-inch spikes of pink flowers over silver leaves. Blooms in May.

'Smokey Rose' AGM (Terra Nova 1997) ('Pewter Veil' × 'Strawberry Swirl').
One of the few hairy-leaved heucheras to do well in the American South, where most pink-flowered heucheras do poorly. The flowers are a soft rose. The foliage is a smokey gray with lighter markings. Plate 83.

'Snow Angel' (Hamernik 1997).
A lovely and strong variegated sanguinea type. Foot-tall mounds of foliage give rise to 20-inch spikes of pink flowers in summer. Appears to be quite hardy and is very popular in the United States. Plate 84.

'Snowflakes' (Blooms).
Listed as early as 1939 and reintroduced in 1950, this cultivar freely produces 20-inch flower spikes of pure white and has a looser habit than many. Does well in containers and in the rock garden, where it has proven to be quite drought-tolerant. Participated in the 1938 RHS Wisley Trials.

'Souvenir de Wolley-Dod' (aka 'Souvenir de C. Wolley-Dod').
The first mention we have been able to find is in the Lemoine et Fils catalog of 1927; we have not been able to pin down an exact time for this cultivar, but all indications are that it originated in the early twentieth century as a tribute to Charles Wolley-Dod made by the apparent raiser of the plant, Lloyd Edwards. May-to-June bloomer with turkey-red flowers on 20-inch spikes, suggesting sanguinea heritage. Green heart-shaped leaves in 9-inch mounds. In current trials at RHS Wisley.

'Sparkler' (Blooms 1950).
'Brizoides' type with open spikes of carmine flowers sold by Blooms. Leaves are well silvered. This cultivar does well in containers and in the rock garden, where it has proven to be quite drought-tolerant.

'Sparkling Burgundy' (Terra Nova 2005).
Burgundy-colored foliage literally glows all spring and summer. This beauty, one of Dan's Top 5, pushes up clean white flowers in spring. The evergreen leaves darken in winter. Forms a medium-sized mound that is great in the

landscape or in containers. Fourteen inches wide and 7 inches tall, with flower spikes to 16 inches. Plate 85.

'Splendour' HC 1955, AM 1959 (Blooms 1950) (NCCPG National Collection). A salmon-flowered 'Brizoides' type sold by Blooms. It has compact habit with foliage to 10 inches high. Strong flower spikes are 20 inches long and adorned by delft-rose flowers. The plant is said to be weak.

'Starry Night' (Terra Nova 2005).
Voluptuous dark leaves and prolific, bicolored blooms: beginning with a major flush in spring, 'Starry Night' offers 14-inch spikes, each holding one to two hundred pink buds that open to white flowers. Great in containers or borders. Plant habit is mounding and compact. Expect some rebloom throughout the summer.

'Sterling Silver' (van den Top 2003).
It appears to have strong americana blood, looking like a seedling of *H. americana* 'Eco-magnifolia'. Rounded and lobed silver leaves with purple veining are said to like sun or light shade. Plants have insignificant flowers and spread to 16 inches. Plate 86.

'Stormy Seas' (Terra Nova 1996) ('Pewter Veil' × ruffled seedling [*H. americana* × *H. micrantha* 'Ridges']).
This is one of Dan's Top 5 and the best landscape heuchera, in his opinion. It has lovely form and vigor, and robust, ruffled foliage with an appliqué of silver, lavender, pewter, and charcoal-gray—dark gray waves smashing into the seashore come to mind (hence the name). Combine with Japanese painted fern and dark-foliaged *Eupatorium rugosum* 'Chocolate' for a lovely color echo. Plate 87.

'Strawberries and Cream' (Terra Nova / Just Must 1999).
Just in time for Wimbledon. This cultivar, a variegated form of 'Strawberry Swirl', occurred in tissue culture and is distributed by Just Must Perennials in England. See 'Strawberry Swirl' for flower description.

'Strawberry Candy' (Terra Nova 1999) (*H. cylindrica* var. *alpina* × 'Magic Wand').
This remarkable plant was a true standout in Terra Nova Trials. Even though

its foliage is compact, the overall spread and visual impact of the huge pink blooms are outstanding. Foliage is green marbled with silver. A rebloomer and therefore good for containers. Plate 88.

'Strawberry Swirl' (Terra Nova 1996) (*H. micrantha* 'Ruffles' × best, most floriferous sanguinea seedling).
Wavy and silvered foliage, with sixty flower stalks on a two-year-old plant, each stalk with hundreds of pink flowers that are much larger than *H. sanguinea* and teardrop-shaped as well. The plant is also twice as large as *H. sanguinea* with excellent hybrid vigor. Has better foliage and deeper pink flowers than 'Pink Ruffles', which it replaced. Plate 89.

'Sunset' (Blooms 1953, aka 'Glow') (NCCPG National Collection).
A sanguinea type that is a later bloomer with large red flowers on 20-inch spikes. Not a strong plant, however.

Super Hybrids. In 1997, a British seed company launched this seed strain with very limited distribution. Said to be taller and more free-flowering than the Bressingham Hybrids. Mostly *H. sanguinea* crosses and selections.

'Susanna' (Rancho Santa Ana Botanic Garden) (*H. maxima* × *H. sanguinea*).
Hybridized by Lee W. Lenz. A sibling to 'Santa Ana Cardinal', this dark red-flowered form is not as tall as its sibling at 18 to 24 inches, but it is just as drought- and shade-tolerant, with similar hardiness.

'Swirling Fantasy' PPAF (Wijnhout 2001).
Evergreen, purpled foliage with rose-red flowers. Nineteen-inch flower spikes from May to July. Derived from Terra Nova stock. Assigned to Witteman, B.V.

'Tall Girl' (Wijnhout 1997).
Thirty-inch spikes of chartreuse flowers over green leaves. Blooms in May and June.

'Tango' (Terra Nova 2005).
Hot fuchsia-pink flowers inspired this hybrid's Latinismo name. This compact plant features purplish leaves with a metallic veil. Great as a specimen or in the border. Foliage mound is 8 inches tall and 14 inches wide, with flower stalks to 20 inches. One of the Dance series from Terra Nova. Plate 90.

'Tattletale' (Wijnhout 1997).
Twenty-inch spikes of clear pink flowers over green leaves. Blooms in May and June.

'Tinian Bronze' (Primrose Path 1997).
This selection by Charles Oliver has large, solid dark bronze leaves and flowers like tiny pinkish pearls on 24-inch stems in early summer. Unlike many bronze-foliaged selections, it retains its dark color through the summer.

'Titania' (Lemoine 1910) (NCCPG National Collection).
This Lemoine introduction was sold by Blooms in the 1950s. An old but vigorous cultivar with salmon-pink flowers on 24-inch stalks. Given to the National Collection by Friesland Staudengarten in 1987. Said to bloom twice in a season and to have sanguinea heritage.

'Toto' (Wijnhout 1997).
Twenty-four-inch spikes of red flowers over green leaves. Blooms in May and June.

'True Love' (Wijnhout 1997).
Thirty-inch spikes with cream flowers over brown leaves. Blooms in May and June.

'Twister' (Wijnhout 1997).
Twelve-inch spikes with cream flowers over brown leaves. Blooms in May.

'Van Gogh'.
Green flowers appear on 20-inch spikes over silvered foliage with purple venation. Leaves mature to a darker purple.

'Veil of Passion' (Terra Nova 1999) ('Velvet Night' × best sanguinea rebloomer).
A darkly veiled heuchera with pink flowers, the first plant offered by Terra Nova that combines veiling and heavy blooming in one cultivar. This early-flowering hybrid just can't wait to bust out of the gate come spring. In horse racing terms, it's a sprinter as well as a stayer—not only a prolific but a constant bloomer, its vigor underlined by the fact that it also flowers well in partial shade.

'Velvet Cloak' (Brown 1999).
Large maroon-black leaves, insignificant flowers. "Not very special," says Bob
Brown somewhat disingenuously of this gift from a customer.

'Velvet Night' (Terra Nova 1995).
This cross between 'Ruby Veil' and 'Pewter Veil' yielded a very dark form,
whose 7-inch slate-black leaves have complex metallic purple overlays. Shimmering puckered leaves. Flowers are on 23-inch stalks and are not significant.
Plate 91.

'Venus' (Witteman 2002).
Evergreen silver-green foliage with a pale green edge and dark green veins.
Insignificant flowers. Twenty-two-inch spikes. Blooms from May to July.

'Vesuvius' (Terra Nova 2000) ('Cherries Jubilee' × *H. sanguinea* 'Best Red').
Number 1 in the 2000 Terra Nova Trials: as Dan describes it, "Profuse and reblooming spires erupt like fountains of magma over the purpled flanks of this
hot little number." Spikes are 16 inches tall. This plant forms thick mounds in
the sun and blooms very well in fifty-five percent shade. Plate 92.

villosa **'Autumn Bride'** (Bluemount Nursery 1994).
A named selection by Martha Pindale of Maryland from a long-cultivated
species. White flowers, like bottlebrushes, hover 2 feet over large round green
leaves. The tall inflorescence blooms unusually late, coming in September.
Prefers half-sun. It is a very decent cut flower.

villosa **'Biddulph Brown'.**
"Later flowering, brownish-red glossy leaves and lots of good small white
flowers from dark stems in tiered columnar heads from August to October,"
says Bob Brown of Cotswold Garden Flowers in his catalog.

villosa **'Chantilly'** (Detriché 2000).
A selection of *H. villosa* 'Crème de la Crème' made by Jacques Detriché of La
Grange aux Vivaces in Chanteloup, France. Foamy, pure white panicles of
flowers resemble *la crème Chantilly*, a kind of a whipped cream. Flower spikes
are 18 to 24 inches tall. Blooms in late summer to early autumn.

villosa **'Crème de la Crème'** (Spruyt).
A very floriferous, late-flowering cultivar with 24-inch sprays of creamy white flowers.

villosa **'Discolor'** (Invalid Name 1985).
This charming plant was seen briefly in the mid 1980s but was somehow lost to horticulture. It had large green leaves with purple undersides, which coloration can also be found in seedling batches grown from *H. villosa* f. *purpurea* and in 'Sashay'. Flower spikes are 18 to 24 inches tall.

villosa **'Emperor's Cloak'.**
Puckered purple leaves with a fuzzy finish give rise to frothy white flowers in July. Sometimes sold as a seed strain, this plant can be variable, producing green seedlings as well. Do try to use the purple seedlings.

villosa **'Melkweg'** (Spruyt 1997).
A seedling selection from Jan Spruyt of Buggenhout, Belgium. Free-flowering creamy white flowers are carried 24 inches over large round green leaves. Prefers half-sun and blooms in July and August. Plate 94.

villosa f. *purpurea* **'Bronze Wave'** (Primrose Path 2000).
This dark-leaved cultivar is the largest heuchera Charles Oliver grows. The wavy-margined hairy leaves are 6 to 8 inches across and make a clump about 24 inches across and 18 inches high. Twenty-four-inch wands of pinkish white flowers are produced from mid to late summer. The plants offered by Primrose Path are of a clone selected for vigor, habit, leaf shape, and retention of good foliage color through the season.

villosa f. *purpurea* **'Palace Purple'** AGM (1980, aka *micrantha* var. *diversifolia* 'Palace Purple').
Certainly among the most popular foliage plants of the 1980s and a true gateway plant toward the acceptance of *Heuchera* as a premier foliage genus, it was named Perennial Plant of the Year in 1991 by the Perennial Plant Association. The select form came from a packet of American Rock Garden Society seeds from pteridologist and botanist Edgar T. Wherry (1885–1982); these were germinated by Brian Halliwell and planted in the Queen's Palace Garden at the Royal Botanic Gardens, Kew. Ensuing seed strains diluted the original

flavor of this once vigorous, dark purple plant, replacing it with pallid, weaker plants that often reverted to green forms. These appear to be less sun-tolerant as well, turning to a very ugly pile of burned leaves by season's end. The original plant has been restored in the clonal selection of Blooms of Bressingham's Bressingham Bronze ('Absi') and Allen Bush's 'Molly Bush', and seed currently offered by Jelitto are of a superior heritage.

The question of parentage has been a hot topic of debate. It's all between *Heuchera micrantha* (of which we have never seen a purple form) and *H. villosa* f. *purpurea* (which is itself a purple form). Charles Oliver feels that 'Palace Purple' is not *H. micrantha* at all because *H. micrantha* is not hardy in Pennsylvania and *H. villosa* is. Furthermore Wherry was not collecting plants in the wild on the west coast of North America, where *H. micrantha* is native, but in the American South, where *H. villosa* is native. Oliver claims that *H. villosa* f. *purpurea* is the same as 'Palace Purple', although there are different forms in the wild. The final nail in the *H. micrantha* vs. *H. villosa* f. *purpurea* coffin is that of Oliver's microscopic examination of the seed coats of different *Heuchera*: spiny seed coats are typical of *H. villosa* and bumpy seed coats are typical of *H. micrantha*. Seed from 'Palace Purple' have a spiny seed coat. Enough said!

villosa f. purpurea 'Royal Red' (Chatto / RHS Wisley List 1997).
Maple-shaped leaves of a rich mahogany-red are formed in low mounds. Shade-tolerant. Eighteen-inch spikes of flowers.

'Virginal' (Lemoine 1904) (NCCPG National Collection).
No further information available.

'Wendy' (Rancho Santa Ana Botanic Garden 1984).
The cross was made by Lee W. Lenz in 1953; the plant was selected by John Farmar Bowers (of Skylark Nursery) and named by John Dourley (RSABG staff) in 1984. Showy pink-flowered form, large upright flowers. Drought- and shade-tolerant. Plate 96.

'Wendy Hardy' (Roderick 1983).
Blooms in early May. "Airy sprays of deep pink flowers May to July," says the Cotswold Garden Flowers catalog. Twenty-inch spikes. A gift from and raised by Wayne Roderick. Primrose Upward recommends it as a "lovely and distinctive selection."

'Weserlachs' (Junge 1957).
Neither 'Weerlachs' as listed in *The RHS Dictionary of Gardening* nor 'Wesserlachs', as listed in some catalogs. Of probable 'Brizoides' genes, it flowers in midsummer; tall, strong spikes of salmon-pink flowers grow to 30 inches tall. Donated to the RHS Wisley Trials by German breeder Ernst Pagels.

'Whirlwind' (Terra Nova 1998) ('Purple Petticoats' × [*H. micrantha* 'Ridges' × *H. sanguinea*]).
Terra Nova's first crumpled, tightly ruffled form to have soft pink flowers. The foliage is very dark purple in spring and fades to lighter tones by late summer in response to more sun and increased photosynthesis. Very drought-resistant and tough.

'White Giant' (1932).
Offered in the Blooms catalog of 1939, 'White Giant' was said to be the tallest, strongest white of the time with 36-inch flower spikes. It is another possible 'Pruhoniciana' selection.

'White Marble' (Primrose Path 1995) (*H. pubescens* × *H. sanguinea* 'White Cloud').
The seed parent was derived from a wild collection of *H. pubescens* made in the shale barrens of Mineral County, West Virginia. In the subsequent seedling batch, Charles Oliver noticed a particularly white-marbled individual, which he named 'Marble-leaf' (Oliver contributed seed of this plant to the 1990 North American Rock Garden Society seed exchange as accession no. 2497, and to the 1992 seed exchange as no. 3064); this 'Marble-leaf' he planted in a stock bed next to the floriferous *H. sanguinea* 'White Cloud', the pollen parent of 'White Marble'. Certainly one of Oliver's best breeding results, with ultra-tough pubescens blood coupled with masses of good-sized ivory flowers, flushed pink, on strong stems to 2 feet. The foliage is silvered and marbled. The fact that it is very drought-tolerant and floriferous makes it an ideal candidate for commercial landscaping. It has proven to be very resistant to leaf scorch and is hardy to at least Zone 3.

'White Spires' (Terra Nova 1997).
One of Terra Nova's early crosses with *H. micrantha* 'Ruffles'. It is more refined and more floriferous, with taller spikes of white flowers. Foliage is less ruffled. Needs full sun for best growth. Plate 97.

'Widar' (Weibull, aka 'Vidar').
Swedish seedsman and breeder Widar Weibull named this introduction, seemingly a stabilized selection of a seed strain from 'Brizoides', for himself. The plant offers cool green foliage and flowers that are a gorgeous scarlet on tall spikes. Seems to be ever-blooming and early blooming as well. Did fairly well at the Penn State Trials in 1998. Several seed companies offer it as a seed strain.

'William How' (NCCPG National Collection).
Obtained from Goatcher's Nursery in 1980. The originator was a customer of Goatcher's who wanted wider distribution. Listed in Trehane's *Index Hortensis*, but no other information is available.

'Winkfield' (Ramsdale) (*H. villosa* f. *purpurea* 'Palace Purple' × 'Sunset').
Mary Ramsdale named this introduction after her home. Dark green, bronzed leaves and good red flowers with a vigorous flowering habit.

'Winter Red' (Primrose Path 1996) (*H. pubescens* × red-flowered 'Brizoides').
This Charles Oliver selection is a sibling to 'Larenim Queen'. Scalloped leaves, delightfully red-rimmed in winter. Large, rich pink flowers are carried on 28-inch spikes for a long period in spring. Excellent form and constitution. Ironically, the plant did very well in many other locales but not for Oliver at his nursery in southwestern Pennsylvania. Plate 98.

'Yellow Dream' (Wijnhout 1999).
Aart Wijnhout himself selected this form from an open-pollinated planting derived from Terra Nova varieties. Yellow-green flowers are carried on spikes that are 28 inches tall. Foliage is green. Blooms in June and July.

'Yeti' (Wijnhout 1997).
Eighteen-inch spikes of white bell-shaped flowers are held over a decorative mound of rounded, deeply cordate, shallow-lobed foliage, mottled green and white. Blooms in June and July.

'Zabeliana' (Zabel 1903).
This old European cultivar, descended from *H. sanguinea* and *H. pilosissima*, was introduced by Hermann Zabel (1832–1912), director of the Royal Garden in Muenden, Germany. At first it was believed to be a species and listed as *H. rosea* Zabel (*The Garden* 13:256, 1907), and later as 'Zabelliana' (*Garden Chron-*

icles 77:437, 1925); however, "Collections de Pleine Terre" of 1909 listed 'Zabeliana' along with 'Edge Hall', 'Rosamonde', and *H. sanguinea* 'Walker's Variety'. The true plant, which had rosy pink flowers on 2- to 3-foot spikes (some later reports attribute flowers of greeny yellow), may no longer be in existence. Plate 99.

CHAPTER 6

Heucherellas (Foamy Bells)

×*Heucherella* (hoy-ker-EL-uh—the math × is not pronounced) is an intergeneric hybrid between *Heuchera* and *Tiarella*. The first ×*Heucherella* cross was made in France in 1912 by Émile Lemoine, who crossed his *Heuchera* 'Brizoides' with *Tiarella cordifolia* to produce ×*Heucherella tiarelloides* (or, as he named it, *Heuchera tiarelloides*); eighty-one years later, in 1993, the Royal Horticultural Society bestowed upon it an Award of Garden Merit (AGM).

Morphologically and physiologically, these plants lie somewhere between the two genera. The leaves have more substance than *Tiarella* but less than *Heuchera*; the flowers too are in the middle, as is the blooming period. Other foliage characteristics are picked up from both parents; often color is picked up from *Heuchera* and form (cut-leaf, fig-leaf) from *Tiarella*. Ruffling and running (stoloniferous) habit do not seem to be transferred, but the central patch of heucherellas derived from newer *Tiarella* cultivars does seem to be dominant.

All forms are sterile and are thus profuse and repeat bloomers. Seed tries to form in the pods, but they quickly shrivel up and do not develop. Attempts to use ×*Heucherella* pollen have failed, as have attempted embryo rescues (a process used widely with lilies, where only partial pollination takes place). The crowns of foamy bells can be divided in early spring with good results. There is not as much "meat" as, for example, with *Heuchera sanguinea*; rooting is slower, therefore, and the divisions need to be watched more closely.

Cultivation follows *Heuchera* more than *Tiarella*. Fluffy, composted soil with adequate moisture yet good drainage is best. Winter wet can be a problem, so absolute drainage is preferred. Morning sun and afternoon shade (especially recommended in the American Southeast and Northeast) will also keep foamy bells happy, resulting in plants that are both more compact and more floriferous.

Charles Oliver reports that heucherellas don't do well in full sun in southwestern Pennsylvania during the summer (Dan bets this would hold true everywhere except in western Europe and in maritime climes from Oregon to

Alaska). Oliver says heucherellas in the Northeast have a problem with summer dieback, even in shade: the central crown goes out, and what's left are little pieces around the edge; he has trialed a lot of promising plants in the last few years and has discarded almost all of them because of this problem. Perhaps different breeding will help. Oliver, for example, is using *Heuchera bracteata* as a parent with *Tiarella* in an attempt to produce a heucherella with different virtues of hardiness, size, and appearance. Terra Nova too has been mixing species to come up with stronger plants.

Certainly the trialing of ×*Heucherella* is far from over; the benefits of these lovely intergeneric crosses are numerous, and ×*Heucherella* will surely continue to evolve in the hands of hybridizers, who have done a fine job so far, as the following list of current cultivars shows.

'Bridget Bloom' (Blooms 1955) (*Heuchera* 'Freedom' × *Tiarella wherryi*). Named after Alan Bloom's eldest daughter, this early cross was performed by Percy Piper at Bloom's suggestion. The result was a vigorous plant with ivy-like green leaves with a central patch and heavy blooming of light pink flowers on 14-inch stalks in June and sporadically in fall. More compact than other heucherellas. Takes full sun to partial shade. It is still a good-selling plant from the Blooms collection. Plate 101.

'Burnished Bronze' (Terra Nova 1999). A cross of *Tiarella* 'Iron Butterfly' and the dark-leaved *Heuchera* 'Breeder's Choice' produced this plant, with large cut leaves and a glossy, dark burnished bronze finish. Add starry, pink flowers on 18-inch branched stalks, and you have an amazing specimen that, in the 2000 Terra Nova Trials, really impressed visitors with its size, flower longevity, and bloom period. Plate 102.

'Checkered White' (Oliver 1998) (*Heuchera* 'Quilter's Joy' × *Tiarella wherryi*). This remains one of the largest heucherellas Oliver has seen, with large white flowers in a cone-shaped inflorescence to 24 inches and checkered light gray and dark green foliage. The foliage and habit of the plant are very similar to *Heuchera*; the flower structure is intermediate. Plate 103.

'Chocolate Lace' (Terra Nova 2001) (*Heuchera* 'Breeder's Choice' × *Tiarella* 'Iron Butterfly'). This introduction is distinct for having the most-cut leaves of any heucherella, with a foliage color that can be described as milk chocolate. The light pink flowers, typically intermediate in form, are carried on 19-inch spikes. Plate 104.

'Cinnamon Bear' (Terra Nova 1999) (*Heuchera* 'Silver Shadows' × *Tiarella* 'Cygnet' PP11051).
This curious plant sports large, cinnamon-brown foliage with two main growth tips, looking a bit like a teddy bear. Tawny flowers are star-like on 18-inch stalks.

'Cranberry Ice' (Terra Nova 1999) (*Tiarella* 'Pink Pendant' × *Heuchera sanguinea*).
A wild color for these hybrids—cranberry-pink tips head the 16-inch salmon-pink flower spikes. Flowers are star-like. Foliage is very attractive: palmate green leaves with brown centers, bronze winter color.

'Crimson Clouds' (Terra Nova 1995).
A sport found in a large planting of ×*Heucherella*. Noted for its unusual leaves, which have burgundy ("crimson") stippling across the leaf and a venation pattern reminiscent of two leaves being fused together ("clouds"). The flowers are pink and up to 18 inches tall.

'Dayglow Pink' (Terra Nova 1999) (*Heuchera* 'Breeder's Choice' × *Tiarella* 'Spring Symphony').
The greatest thrill in hybridizing is to hit a color breakthrough, and, as Dan exclaims, "'Dayglow Pink' came through with flying colors!" This hybrid stunned him from the day its brilliant pink flowers first bloomed on branched stalks to 12 inches tall. Leaves are cut with a chocolate inlay and form 8-inch mounds. Excellent habit and vigor. Plate 105.

'Earth Angel' (Terra Nova 1997) (*Heuchera americana* 'Eco-magnififolia' × *Tiarella* 'Pink Pendant').
This is a sister seedling to 'Viking Ship' and 'Silver Streak'. Sixteen-inch spikes hold large ivory flowers. Flowers are star-like. Foliage is very attractive: palmate and light brown. Color is more intense in spring.

'Gold' (Terra Nova 2005).
This heucherella was chosen by Proven Winners to star in their Strike It Rich

series. Deeply cut golden "stars" with sharply cut lobes adorn this selection. The plant is compact, with tightly overlapping leaves in the spring. The mound height is only 5 inches, and the spread is 12 inches. Pale cream flowers are on 12-inch spikes.

'Heart of Darkness' (Oliver 2004).
Eighteen-inch spikes bear foamy flowers over tricolored foliage: maroon over a silver-gray patch over green. Colors will vary with the seasons.

'Kimono' (Terra Nova 1999) (*Heuchera* 'Green Spice' × *Tiarella* 'Pink Pendant').
Inspired by the colorful cloaks of Japan, 'Kimono', like 'Viking Ship', exhibits narrow, ornamented foliage in spring and huge, much rounder palmate leaves in summer; its silvers, purples, and greens are indescribably ornate. Tawny flowers on 18-inch spikes. Tony Avent of Plant Delights Nursery was simply blown away by this plant when he came out on tour. Wonderful metallic rose winter color. Plate 106.

'Pearl Shadows' (Oliver 2000) (unnamed *Heuchera* Larenim Hybrids clone × *Tiarella* 'Braveheart').
This clone offers pink flowers on 18-inch stems and a dark maroon heart and silvery overlay on green leaves, but it has not proved vigorous and will be replaced.

'Pink Frost' (Primrose Path 1989) (pink-flowered *Heuchera* 'Brizoides' × *Tiarella wherryi*).
This selection by Charles Oliver was introduced by Primrose Path as 'Tinian Pink', marketed by Terra Nova in 1994 as 'Pink Frost', and thereafter listed under that name by Primrose Path. Lovely frosted foliage and soft pink blooms on 18-inch stalks. A beauty with extended flowering and taller scapes than 'Rosalie'. Foliage clumps are 5 inches high.

'Pink Gem' (Terra Nova 2005).
This plant was chosen by Proven Winners as a member of their Strike It Rich series. Star-like leaves are painted in layers, with purple centers over silvery frosting over green. Clouds of barely pink flowers finish the picture. The foliage mound is 8 inches tall and 16 inches wide. Flower stalks are well branched and 18 inches tall in profuse masses.

'Quicksilver' PP11081 (Oliver 1997) (unnamed sibling of *Heuchera* 'Quilter's Joy' × *Tiarella wherryi*).

A compact clumping plant featuring bronze foliage with a pronounced silver metallic overlay between veins. White flowers arise from pinkish buds on 18-inch, dark flowering stems from late spring to midsummer. This highly lauded foamy bells won a first prize at the Royal Society for Horticulture Perennial Plant Exposition in September 1997 in Lisse, The Netherlands, and is the most vigorous and enduring heucherella in Oliver's trials in southwestern Pennsylvania.

'Rosalie' (Huber 1983) (*Heuchera* 'Prairie Fire' × seedling of *Tiarella cordifolia* subsp. *marmorata*).

The flowers are more compact than those of many heucherellas, but the plant is susceptible to mildew. Tony Huber, now retired, was a breeder at Norseco Seeds in Montreal, Canada. Plate 108.

'Silver Streak' (Terra Nova 1997) (*Heuchera americana* 'Eco-magnififolia' × *Tiarella* 'Pink Pendant').

This was a revolutionary plant, using parents that were very different from those involved in previous hybrids. Palm-shaped leaves are overlaid with silver and purple; profuse white flowers kissed with lavender are carried on 20-inch spikes. Reblooming can occur into fall. Foliage clumps are 6 inches tall. Plate 109.

'Snow White' (Primrose Path 1989) (pink-flowered *Heuchera* 'Brizoides' × *Tiarella wherryi*).

This Charles Oliver selection, a sibling to 'Pink Frost', was introduced by Primrose Path in 1989 as 'Tinian White', marketed by Terra Nova in 1994 as 'Snow White', and thereafter listed under that name by Primrose Path. Green foliage gives rise to numerous white blooms on 18-inch stalks; foliage clumps are 5 inches high. Shows extended flowering and taller scapes than 'Rosalie' or 'Bridget Bloom'.

'Stoplight' (Terra Nova 2004) (*Heuchera* 'Best Gold Seedling' × *Tiarella* 'Pirate's Patch').

This seedling caught Dan's eye with the first few leaves out. The rounded shocking-yellow leaves are overlaid with a large dark red patch. Flowers are creamy white and are on 18-inch spikes. Foliage clumps are 12 inches wide and 6 inches tall. Plate 110.

'Storm Clouds' (Oliver 1994) ([unnamed F$_1$ of *Heuchera* 'White Marble' × *H.* 'Montrose Ruby'] × *Tiarella wherryi*).
This looked very good in Oliver's trials, but stock went into a decline the year after its introduction, and the selection was replaced with 'Quicksilver'. Oliver does not have stock anymore, though he thinks that Nancy Goodwin does. She has indicated that it has done well for her. It is similar in coloration to 'Quicksilver' but not as silvery and with neither the vigor nor the fullness of foliage and habit.

'Sunspot' (Terra Nova 2002) (*Heuchera* 'Breeder's Choice' × *Tiarella* 'Spring Symphony').
A brilliant selection of 'Dayglow Pink' with electric-yellow foliage and blood-red center patches. Pink flowers, identical to 'Dayglow Pink'. Blooms just as well, too. Color fades to a straw-yellow in summer. One of Terra Nova's most popular plants. Fourteen inches wide and 7 inches tall in leaf. Flower spikes are 16 inches tall. Plate 111.

tiarelloides AGM (Lemoine 1912).
This was the granddaddy of them all, a cross of a pink-flowered form of *Heuchera* 'Brizoides' and *Tiarella cordifolia* made by Émile Lemoine. Leaves are heuchera-like, green with small flecks of burgundy. Soft pink flowers rise on 16-inch stalks. Calyx fused into a small cup. Flowers are not as dense as other cultivars. Stoloniferous. Hardy to Zone 5.

tiarelloides **'Alba'** (Lemoine 1925).
The result of a cross between a white-flowered *Heuchera* 'Brizoides' and *Tiarella wherryi*. Similar in every respect to ×*Heucherella tiarelloides* except for the flower color and the fact that it is not stoloniferous. In a letter to William Stearn, Émile Lemoine wrote that he used *Tiarella cordifolia* in the cross, but upon examination and trialing of the plants that were sent him in May of 1939, Stearn determined that the tiarella in question had to be *T. wherryi* because of its nonstoloniferous habit. Thus Stearn became the "author" of this plant (and, later, the great innovator and organizer of horticultural nomenclature). Hardy to Zone 5.

'Viking Ship' (Terra Nova 1997) (*Heuchera americana* 'Eco-magnififolia' × *Tiarella* 'Pink Pendant').

More than just a breakthrough, 'Viking Ship' is a new plant form. It possesses silvered leaves in spring that sport detached leaflets, something that is seen in only one other genus, *Trevesia*; these fill in to silvered maple-like leaves for the summer months. Strong pink spires of star-like flowers ascend to 18 inches. The spikes branch, prolonging the season with their blooms. Tolerant of sun, shade, and humidity. Plate 112.

'White Blush' (Primrose Path 1993) (pink-flowered *Heuchera* 'Brizoides' × *Tiarella wherryi*).

This Charles Oliver selection, another sibling to 'Pink Frost' and 'Snow White', was introduced as 'Tinian White Blush' in 1993 by Primrose Path and then listed from 1994 on as 'White Blush'. Ivy-like foliage gives rise to 16-inch spikes of creamy white blooms blushed with soft pink. Foliage clumps are 5 inches high.

CHAPTER 7

Culture and Care

To grow a plant, one must know its origins—see it in the wild and know the seasons it experiences there. To know a plant is to work alongside a plant, to live with it, observing its own seasons of foliage and bloom, analyzing the soil it grows in, recording the rainfall it receives. To grow a plant is to know a plant. Different *Heuchera* species live on mountain passes in gravelly scree, in desert sand, on moist rock walls, and in woodland. While it is easy to settle on a specific suitable potting medium for species, one that is based on where and how they grow in the wild, hybrid heucheras can change their soil preferences. We must therefore compose our soil mix so that it suits what most heucheras demand: perfect drainage, acidic pH, and moderate moisture retention.

In the garden

Ever since heucheras evolved in the Cordilleran Rockies, they have wanted drainage, which assures the proper exchange of oxygen and carbon dioxide as well as minerals and micronutrients. Their ancestors grew in crevices, fine volcanic detritus, and the like; it is only logical that drainage remains essential to their happiness. In an ideal garden situation, heucheras would be planted on a slight incline so that drainage would be assured and a sandy loam would be supplemented with organic matter (like rotted bark or compost). Coarse sand (not fine, beach sand) is the key. The americana hybrids take loamy and clay soils better than many other hybrids, especially the sanguinea types, but they should still have adequate drainage around the crown. Clay soils need to be sharply amended with grit, large-particle organic matter, and gypsum to increase tilth; simply adding sand can turn clay into concrete. It is sometimes wiser to go above a clay layer with a raised bed of amended soil.

Heucheras prefer cool night temperatures. The warmer the summer nights, the more critical drainage becomes: it is vital that extra drainage be used in the

Deep South. Some unadapted heucheras will succumb to the high heat and humidity of the Deep South by staying in a state of suspended animation until the nights cool down. Fertilizer must not be applied to plants in these conditions, as they cannot process the food and can actually be killed by this treatment.

Heucheras are good neighbors in that they are not (with the exception of *Heuchera micrantha* var. *macropetala*) stoloniferous, and they help to retain moisture in the surrounding soil whether it is loamy or sandy. Amendment to the depth and width of an American shovel is adequate for starting off one-gallon potted plants even in poorer soils. Do test your soil for pH. While heucheras are said to grow in soils of pH 8.5, they are happiest in a pH range of 5.8 to 6.3.

In containers

The current craze of container gardening is at fever pitch, and heucheras are among the very best perennials to grow in containers. Why? They are evergreen, they have year-round interest (people marvel over the foliage when kissed by hoarfrost in the winter; the ruffled forms are especially showy), they are quite drought-resistant (their large rhizome, besides serving as a source of starch, stores water), and they do not overwhelm the container. English designer Malcolm Hillier was among the first to employ the hybrid heucheras in this way (see his *The Book of Container Gardening*, 1991). Hillier casts *Heuchera villosa* f. *purpurea* 'Palace Purple' as the star in a zestful perennial semi-shade combination, along with *Houttuynia cordata* 'Chameleon' and *Tolmiea menziesii* (a country cousin to *Heuchera*). He also recommends *Hosta montana* 'Aureomarginata' and *Leucothoe fontanesiana* 'Rainbow' as prime companions to other purple-leaved heucheras for a long-lasting and colorful mélange.

In the average-sized container, it might be easier to use the smaller hybrids, especially those by Charles Oliver. His aptly named 'Coral Bouquet' would be ideal with some of the silvery helichrysums, and the Petite series, particularly 'Petite Pearl Fairy,' seems to have been made for life in a terra-cotta pot.

The container itself must have adequate drainage. Most containers have drain holes that are too tiny; these should be enlarged by drilling with a mason bit or "nibbled" with a pair of pliers. Crocking (placing old pot shards over the drain hole) is a must. All plants in containers live a confined life. All their needs must be met in a space much smaller than what nature normally provides. Heucheras, which are often denizens of small soil deposits in rock walls, are uniquely adapted to this treatment.

When planting heucheras in a container, make sure you don't use the typical mix, which is peat-heavy. A good soil mix is the key to container success. We recommend the following: 40 percent pumice (or large-grain perlite), 30 percent bark, and 30 percent peat (with a 7:3 proportion of aggregate to peat). To this mix we add a small starter-fertilizer charge with micronutrients (and, in our case, lime, to bring pH up to 5.8 to 6.3: be sure to test your local water supply for Ca levels before adding lime) and a surfactant (for even watering). This mix will dry out faster than annual mixes but will keep the plants stronger and better able to handle the dog days of summer. Time-release fertilizers (described in the next section) can be incorporated at planting time.

When transplanting into containers, *do not* bury the crowns of the plants. This is the single most common mistake, and the most deadly. Match the plug or pot soil-height to the container soil-height, and you will have no problems. In areas with moss, algae, or liverwort problems, a $1/2$-inch layer of pumice can do much to keep these primitive weeds down. A cup of vinegar in a gallon of water can be a reasonable liverwort-killer; spraying the vinegar solution may be just as effective a drench. *Always* "test-treat" a single plant before you do a bunch: vinegar can kill plants, too. Always water plants in after transplanting. Air pockets can kill! Big, elongated heucheras can and should be planted deeper, so long as the crown is kept above the soil.

Heucheras like to be watered and then be allowed to dry out. In Holland, watering is done by journeymen, quite often the most skilled people in the nursery. The opposite is true in the United States, where Dan has seen more damage from overwatering than from drying out. Train yourself to feel the soil—do not be afraid to knock the occasional plant out of the pot to see how well pots are getting watered. Many pots will develop hydrophobic tendencies, especially mixes that are high in bark. "I can't get them wet!" is a familiar cry in midsummer. This may be the time to work some surfactant into the soil by proportioner or by watering can—$1/2$ teaspoon will do several gallons! Dishwashing liquid (just a few drops in a quart of water) will not change pH appreciably but will help these pots take up the water.

Fertilizers

Perennials are *not* annuals. Soluble applications in the 250 to 300 ppm rate (or 1 tablespoon soluble 20-20-20 to the gallon) may be tolerated occasionally, but we prefer a very mild 75 to 100 ppm (1 teaspoon 20-20-20 soluble to the gallon) as a constant feed. Hostas and daylilies can take fertilizer heat, but heuchs and heucherellas cannot. We all know that too much lush growth will inhibit flowering and create a plant that is more difficult to maintain. Lush plants crowd (and kill) smaller plants; they dry out faster and become fertilizer "junkies," needing more than normal amounts of food to support their extra foliage. For most perennials, a moderate growth rate with firm foliage is preferred. Soluble feed can be very variable—nursery professionals need to check their proportioners often for proper dilution.

The advent of time-release fertilizers was a boon for container growing as it is easily mixed into the soil and the slow-release action prevents many of the salt buildups that conventional fertilizers can cause. We prefer to use a slow-release fertilizer in larger containers. We have tried several products in the market, some of which did well until the first week of warm weather, when they "poured on the juice" and just about burned our plants. We prefer to use a polymer-coated product with small particle size—Apex (three-month formulation), for example (McConkey, at 800-426-8124, or your local ag store may carry this product). Fertilizer may be mixed directly into the soil or top-dressed. If it's mixed in, prepare only enough for a potting session, as, with any slow-release fertilizer, salts can build up in soil after time.

Heucheras are not heavy feeders; most have lower rather than greater fertilizer needs. But if you are going to grow them in containers, consider a slow-release fertilizer that is at least four months; we use a three- to four-month 16-5-9 formula with micronutrients plus iron (rates are on the bag). The organic grower might consider using a foliar spray made from either Pacific kelp or Norwegian kelp. Multi-crop seaweed has been getting good reviews from people as well. Organic foliar sprays, such as compost tea, will work well for both the contained and the uncontained heuchera.

Deadheading, maintenance

Dan visited Roger's Gardens in Newport Beach, California, to find, near the pottery section, a huge containerized specimen of 'Stormy Seas' nearly four years old. The basket's chains had rusted, but this yard-wide hybrid heuchera had required no maintenance other than yearly top dressing and removal of old flower stalks once a season. No pruning, no soil replacement . . . "Not bad," Dan thought to himself.

Granted, 'Stormy Seas' is an especially fine landscape heuchera; some other varieties do require resetting or mounding every two years. A heuchera is in need of such a treatment when its rhizome's stems exceed three inches in length. When the stems get too long, high winds and severe cold can destroy the terminal growth tips and open up areas for infection. Remove stem tips with a sharp knife or razor and plunge them into the ground or into potting soil to make more plants; lateral buds will emerge the following spring. Resetting a plant involves "popping" the rootball out of the ground, digging a deeper hole in the same spot or elsewhere, and resetting the plant with 3 inches of soil mulch. It is important not to cover the crown tips, as this may cause rot or death. Some people think it is easier simply to mound 3 inches of mulch over the plant, but we prefer resetting—which is also a good opportunity for dividing the plant and "sharing the wealth" among the garden and friends. Early spring, when the ground thaws, is our preferred time for this operation. Without this treatment, many heucheras show less vigor, less flowers, and less foliage.

Flowering heucheras do benefit from stalk removal after flowering. Do try to remove the stalk at a point very low on the plant to eliminate the "hedgehog" look in winter. Flower stalks come off very cleanly with a proper tug when dry or fresh. As food is stored in the foliage as well as the stems, we recommend that only discolored foliage be removed, in spring, as new growth is just starting to push.

Pests and diseases

Heucheras owe their popularity, in part, to their outstanding resistance to pests and diseases. Plants happily growing in a well-draining, acid soil with decent organic content and moderate moisture are rarely affected by disease and are less attractive to insects. But when one of these elements is not provided, a number of pathogens and nasty creatures are waiting to take over. Before bringing out the heavy-hitter chemicals, we always give the most organic solution a chance. If we see an ailing plant, we put on our detective hats and ask why. Is the soil too wet or dry? Perhaps a simple relocation can solve the problem. Heucheras are extremely resilient and will resprout within an inch of death. Problems with pH are a little harder to discern; a pH of 8.5 and above will be evidenced by such symptoms as lack of growth and chlorotic foliage.

Heuchera rust

Heuchera rust is a disease commonly associated with cooler temperatures in the spring. Symptoms are medium to dark orange-brown pustules on the bottom of the leaf, which, when old enough, show on the top of the leaf as bleached spots. But the pustules are the clear identifying mark and the call to action.

The disease is relatively easy to control in the greenhouse: simply raise the temperatures to above 70F day, and 60F night, for approximately a week; this, when combined with a spray treatment, is usually sufficient. We found it effective first to remove the worst leaves; then clear the infection with Zerotol (hydrogen dioxide), a nontoxic fungicide/bactericide/viricide; then alternate between Contrast, a systemic fungicide that is both an eradicant and a protectant, and a Mancozeb product (also good for mildew). Spectro 90 WDG (a combination of two broad-spectrum fungicides: Cleary's 3336 and Daconil) is also effective in rust attacks. If practicable, eliminate infected leaves to reduce spread of the spores.

This regimen works for most types of rust. All rusts (there are different genera) spread rapidly, and the key to control is scouting and identifying the pathogen before the spots show up on the top of the leaf.

Foliage disorders

Most foliage problems in heucheras are caused by pathogens and environmental circumstances: molds, bacteria, sunburn, nematodes, and chemical burns.

Plants in enclosed spaces with very moist conditions (like a wet greenhouse) may show a "furry" growth of mold (fungus) on old and dead stems and leaves. Under the right conditions this mold (*Botrytis*) can overwhelm healthy tissue. Mildew, another fungus, is an uncommon problem with most heucheras except for *Heuchera sanguinea*, which is very susceptible to attack. Mildew appears as a grayish film that attacks plants that have been stressed and then continues to kill healthy tissue. Benomyl (a systemic benzimidazole fungicide) can be helpful in stopping mildew, as can spraying a mild solution of baking soda, which changes the surface pH of the leaves, disallowing the growth of the fungus. A product called FirstStep (a bactericide) is available to commercial growers for mildew control. Increasing airflow to dry the foliage is always recommended.

Heucheras can be hit by bacteria both above and below ground in less-than-ideal conditions. Heavy clay soils are detested by heucheras, which can rot at the base courtesy of a bacterial infection caused by *Sclerotinia*. Very high humidity, warm summer nights, and wet soil can set the stage for infections by *Thielaviopsis* or *Fusarium* spp. as well. The cure is to reroot the solid parts in sand and provide sharp drainage in the new planting site. Commercial growers can use Cleary's 3336 (50WP) or Domain (thiophanate-methyl 50WP) as a preventative. Dark spots on the leaves surrounded by a yellow halo are evidence of infection by the pathogen *Xanthomonas*; removal of affected foliage and copper sprays like Kocide WP (a copper-based wettable powder) or copper sulfate will help to minimize problems.

Pseudomonas, another bacterial disease, is difficult to control. Symptoms of infection are round spots, burnt orange to brown in color. Treatment is similar to that recommended for rust: remove affected leaves and apply copper-based sprays. Cutting down on overhead watering is also beneficial.

Root weevils and other pests

Overall, *Heuchera* has proven resistant to slugs, spider mites, white flies, and an assortment of other pests. Cutworms may take an occasional nibble, but if there is a nemesis, it's the dreaded strawberry root weevil in the West and the black vine weevil in the East. Root weevils are seen only during evening forages. The insidious evil occurs over winter, when the beetle larvae hatch and channel through the succulent stems. In a severe infestation, the entire top of the plant will fall off when you rake your yard (revealing the cream-colored grubs, laughing at you). Fortunately, heucheras are so tough that we have seen many adventitious roots already sprouting from the decapitated top, which can be replanted in the soil without further ado. There are many types of root weevils, the strawberry root and the black vine weevils being the worst offenders. Sometimes knowing which one you have can be important, because it affects the time of year they emerge and consequently when treatments should occur. Notched edges on the leaves of azaleas and rhododendrons will verify their presence in your garden.

Root weevils are long snouted beetles with very hard shells that are typically brown, black, or reddish. Their larvae are approximately $3/8$ to $1/2$ inch long with tan heads and white C-shaped bodies. Although the adults eat notches on the leaves, the real damage is done by the larvae eating the roots and crown. Control falls into two basic categories. Spraying with synthetic pyrethroids, on early summer evenings, or drenching for larvae in the fall and sometimes spring. Combined control is far more effective.

178

A new pyrethroid, Scimitar, was found effective at Terra Nova and in trials at the university level. Larval control depends heavily upon sufficient saturation of the rhizosphere. We have used predatory nematodes with great success, but a note of caution: soil temperatures *must* be 60F or higher for the organism to be effective. Hence, timing is crucial in the fall. In the Pacific Northwest that means the first week of October, but many regions would want to use mid September as a guide. New varieties available "across the pond" have tolerances down to 40F.

Some baits are effective as a complementary control against root weevils. And Dan has applied hot water (100 to 120F) to the roots and crown of infested plants during the winter; the larvae are killed within two seconds, and the plant "shrugs off" this shock treatment. This requires experimentation but is a very safe method of control.

Heucheras are not immune to leaf nematodes, especially in the southern United States. Nematodes can disfigure the foliage by forming purpled or papery patches between the veins. We have not seen leaf nematodes in the cool

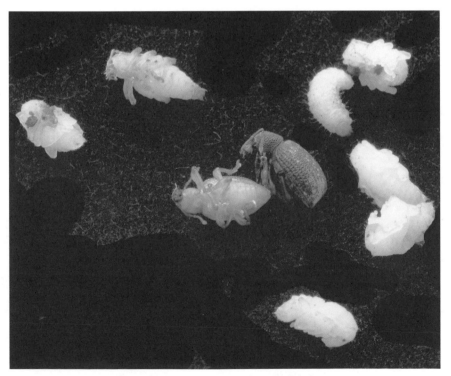

Root weevils in larval, pupal, and adult forms.

Pacific Northwest, but we do know these creatures can be passed from *Hosta* and other genera to *Heuchera*. Control is difficult: either treatments with Zerotol (a sterilant) or nematicides (which are usually not available to retail customers). Prevention is best: become a keen observer of the pest on other plants; do not place your heucheras near susceptible genera, and minimize their exposure to overhead irrigation. Heat treatments can also kill these nasties.

CHAPTER 8

Propagation

Seed

Heucheras are an easy plant to propagate from seed. Like most of the Saxifragaceae, *Heuchera* has very fine seeds; they look like miniature poppy seeds (at $1/100$ scale) and, like poppy seeds, they are black. A little bit goes a *long* way. Some heucheras, especially *H. sanguinea* selections like 'Leuchtkäfer', 'Sioux Falls', and 'White Cloud', are sold as seed strains and are fairly uniform in flower color and foliage. Other strains, such as the Bressingham Hybrids and Super Hybrids, yield a diverse group of flower colors; foliage too may vary, with some plants showing more silver marking ('Jack Frost' is such a plant).

One needs only to understand that seed from a 'Pewter Veil' does not yield another 'Pewter Veil' but rather an aggregate of hybrids and throwbacks to the species involved in the original cross; the chances of having a superior or even equivalent plant, therefore, are thousands to one. In Holland, for instance, Dan toured a quarter-mile row of open-pollinated heucheras (derived from many Terra Nova hybrids) which Aart Wijnhout had grown for Luc Klinkhamer; the variation in progeny was amazing—a collection of purples, metallics, and ruffles in the foliage and flowers in various colors (this seed blend is sold by Jelitto and Thompson and Morgan). Luc offered Dan as many of these plants as he wanted, but after an hour of scrutiny Dan concluded that not one of them was superior to what was created in Terra Nova's breeding program. Some of Terra Nova's introductions are a single selection out of five thousand plants; asexual propagation is the only way to propagate such unique plants.

All heucheras have tiny flowers on long stems that sway in the wind. Brightly colored heuchera flowers with ample nectar are an effective attractant to insects and hummingbirds. Others are wind-pollinated; you will see puffs of pollen fly out with a swift gust. Once the seeds have formed, the long stems serve as an excellent means to distribute the seed. Collect the stems just as the seed heads are dehiscing (separating), place them in an open brown paper bag, and dry them for several days in a warm, dry spot. Carefully remove the stems from the bag, keeping them upright, and gently shake the tiny "salt-shakers" at their tips over a piece of printer paper that has been folded and unfolded twice (once vertically, once horizontally), aiming for the X creased in the middle of the sheet. Refold and label the paper.

Heuchera seed need light and a bit of warmth (70 to 70F) to germinate. Seed can be sown immediately (they will lose much viability in six months); stratification (exposure to an eight-week cold period) is not necessary. You will need the following to germinate heucheras:

- a seed tray (Terra Nova uses 10- by 20-inch trays) with drainage
- a clear cover (plastic or glass)
- a well-drained compost (potting soil should be 30 percent perlite), with a pH of 5.5 to 5.8
- a mister with water
- a sheet of printer paper
- fluorescent light (suspend 6 inches above soil surface) or bright greenhouse
- a heating mat or warm, bright spot to maintain 70F
- a plastic tag (one per variety)

Follow this procedure:

1. Moisten the compost, and let it drain fully.
2. Fold the piece of paper in half.
3. Place a portion of seed in the crease of the paper.
4. Hold the paper 4 to 12 inches above the compost's surface; gently tap the paper while moving it back and forth over the width of the tray. It is deadly to sow too many seed: distribute them over the surface like you were peppering a steak (or tofu, for you vegans out there). Some people mix the seed with sand and *do* use a saltshaker to sow the seed!
5. Mist the compost until fully moist.
6. Label the tray with a plastic tag showing the name of the variety and the date of sowing.
7. Put the clear cover over the tray, and place the tray on the heating mat.
8. Place under bright light and be patient.

Heucheras will germinate in two to three weeks. Once up, with the tiny seed-leaves showing, we remove the clear cover over several days. Whereas watering was self-recirculating in the sealed dome, you must now watch the soil and water when the surface appears barely dry. From these first leaves will sprout a "heuchera-looking" true leaf ⅛ inch wide. Ensuing leaves get progressively larger. We normally transplant at the presentation of the fourth leaf, usually two weeks after the seed-leaves are up. We will usually "pre-dibble" the flat (make small holes in the soil) with a chopstick to a depth of 1 inch. We then transfer to a 72-cell flat using a dibble or a large unwound paperclip to transfer to the soil in the flat. Once gently watered, the flats can be transferred to the lights or the greenhouse. In a week or two, flats can be watered with a dilute fertilizer (¼ strength). When roots reach the bottom of the cell (six weeks or less), transfer plants to larger pots or plant outdoors in mild weather.

Division and cuttings

Heucheras store food in their fleshy stems, which are also marked by other propagation resources. We have found the stems particularly easy to root in

Heuchera cuttings ready to be potted up.

the sanguinea types: we simply snap them off and plunge them in the soil, and they will root and prosper. In the greenhouse or at home, you can fill plug trays or pots with a 1:1 mix of potting soil and perlite and place the stem cuttings in pre-dibbled holes. We find that rooting hormones are not needed, but a fungicidal drench is a good rot-preventative. Some powdered rooting hormones have a fungicide in the mix, and it is simply easier to give the cuttings a quick dip. Once roots hit bottom (in about three weeks at 70F), the plant can be transplanted outdoors. Most montane species can be propagated in the same way. Hybrids involving *Heuchera micrantha* and *H. maxima* are also easy. Problems arise with the *H. americana* group of cultivars; crowns tend to be tighter, with less "meat" than other species, so division by a sharp knife or a pair of pruners is usually in order.

To increase large numbers of a specific heuchera, nurserymen take heel cuttings from the plant. This technique involves following a leaf to the petiole base. If you look hard, you will see a small bud at the base. Taking your sharpest knife, cut this eye out with a $1/4$- to $1/2$-inch strip of the main stem. Do use a fungicidal rooting powder and place in a pre-dibbled 72-cell flat filled with sterile potting soil. Do not bury the cuttings too deeply. Place on a heating mat and cover with a dome, as high humidity is important. Plants must have all (or, for bigger-leaved heuchera, some) of the leaf attached to be successful. Once roots hit bottom (in six weeks), the plants can be shifted to larger pots.

Tissue culture

What do Charles Darwin, salmon sperm, and carrots have to do with tissue culture? Each of these elements has contributed to the understanding and science of growing plants in test tubes. Tissue culture (tc) is a process in which plants are multiplied rapidly under sterile conditions. Even before World War II, scientists using Darwin's research on plant auxins (plant growth regulators) were able to increase carrot cells in vitro (in glass containers). Unfortunately, this brew of sugars, fertilizer salts, rooting hormone, and agar only increased the root mass in the test tube; it didn't increase the number of plants. Scientists had to come up with a way to produce shoots. In an Edisonesque quest, they used "shelf chemistry"—that is, throwing in every chemical on the shelf—to see if they could stimulate shoots. One did: kinetin, an extract derived from autoclaved salmon sperm. When a single sterilized growing tip was placed on a medium containing this extract, shoots sprouted, in some cases forty-fold. From this one clump, forty more test tubes could be started, and six weeks later, sixteen hundred test tubes were lined up in formation. *Millions* of identical plants, or clones, could be produced in a single year. When the crop reached its optimum number, the plants would be placed onto a different medium to induce roots. Once roots were formed, the plants would go into the greenhouse to be planted into soil and weaned. This work, done by Skoog and Murashige (and many others), paved the way for providing the public with plants (even two-thousand-dollar orchids) at an affordable price. "Better living through chemistry" took on new meaning for hortiholics everywhere.

Folks might think that a laboratory, autoclaves, chemicals, scales, mixers, and the like would be a huge investment. Well, they'd be right. However, in this age of five-minute meals, media can be ordered premixed from suppliers like Carolina Biological; a kitchen stove can cook the media; a pressure cooker can sterilize the test tubes. An alcohol burner can sterilize scalpels and forceps, and a dust-free, draft-free environment can produce all the plants

Tissue-cultured *Heuchera* 'Amber Waves'.

you'd ever want. In *Plants from Test Tubes* (1996), Lydiane Kyte gives an excellent overview of the process and delves into building a "home lab." There's even a Web site by Carol M. Stiff specifically geared to the "kitchen culturist": http://www.home.turbonet.com/kitchenculture.

The benefits plants derive from the tissue-culture process are many: plants can be cleared of viruses and bacterial or fungal infections that are passed on by conventional propagation, "juvenility" is instilled, plants are uniform and identical. The upshot of all this is that the plants will grow healthier, stronger, and faster. We've seen heucheras grow three times larger from a 1-inch plug than from a 3-inch cutting in the same time period. If the clone is from a blue flower, you'll get a blue flower—unless a mutation occurs. Every commercial lab has either suffered or benefited from mutation in their cultures. Some facts on mutations: they do not occur too commonly, they can be induced, and they can be worth a lot of money. A number of the unusual heucheras you see are the result of such tissue-culture mutations (Plates 113 and 114).

Take a walk in the park and admire the towering shade trees in their brightest hues, walls of stately and showy rhododendrons, azaleas, and kalmias. Saunter through the neighborhood and see masses of the rarest perennials and baskets of opulent annuals. All the aforementioned plants are commonly propagated by tissue culture. Not only heucheras but hostas, lilacs, daylilies, tiarellas, pulmonarias, and many other perennials are also routinely multiplied with this method. The general outcome of fifty years of tissue culture is that the world now enjoys healthier plants, exceptional plants, in greater variety at an affordable price. Who could argue with that?

CHAPTER 9

Garden Uses and Combinations

It is exhilarating to have a group of plants that can do almost anything you ask of it—which might explain the popularity of *Heuchera*. A marginalized group of "grandmother" plants with little history and stereotypical baggage as recently as the 1980s, heucheras have risen from virtual obscurity to Top 10 prominence in the new millennium. Back in 1994, *Heuchera* hybrids were just beginning to makes waves in gardening circles, but it was hardly the kind of wave you could surf on. In the years since we first decided that a book focusing on the genus was needed, we have seen these plants become a staple in garden designs; we have witnessed their uses expand and their core adaptability in gardens increase. Surf's up!

Rising along with the uptrend in gardening, hybrid heucheras have quickly established their own ground in the ever-changing pantheon of perennials for the temperate garden. They are now routinely utilized—often in original ways—to make both our public and our private gardens beautiful. Their versatility and beauty are recognized all over North America, the United Kingdom, France, The Netherlands, Sweden, Denmark, and Germany as well as in the warmer climates of New Zealand, Australia, and Japan. Tried by a variety of climates and situations, heucheras have come through splendidly. After all, what does the reputation of a beautiful plant matter to the average gardener if the plant be not hardy, adaptable, and an "easy doer" to boot? Fortunately the good name of *Heuchera* survives untarnished, thanks not only to the plant's excellent inherent qualities but to the care with which the hybrids have been selected.

Heucheras (especially the hybrids) give us an array of choices without a lot of demands. Whatever our gardening style—experimental, integrative, creative—we can turn to heucheras, as naturalizer, feature plant, and container plant. Plantsman Dan Hinkley has unreserved admiration for heucheras in yet another capacity, calling their year-round, weed-smothering foliage "the perfect groundcover" (1999 Heronswood Nursery catalog). Heucheras have a primal quality that harmonizes with many settings; this and their ability to provide a continuum of foliage and texture are the chief reasons for their popularity. Often they act as a contrasting foil in combinations that vary with the seasons; this continuity is important because most gardeners want to highlight different plant favorites at different times. In the 1990s everyone was experimenting with heucheras—we heard that Martha Stewart and Rosemary Verey were running around Martha's garden, showy heuchera leaves in hand, considering new combinations against existing plant material.

As Graham Stuart Thomas wrote in *Perennial Garden Plants* (1990), "The value of good foliage cannot be overstated or overestimated; flowers come and go, but the leaves . . . last for the whole season and supplement the floral display." Their range of leaf color and form is precisely what makes heucheras such an exciting subject for the twenty-first-century gardener. Besides the usual greens, we gardeners are given silver-veiled foliage, subtly toned leaves of copper, bronze, purple, chocolate, and soft yellow. Dan recalls a top garden designer picking up a pot of 'Amber Waves', hurriedly holding it to every plant in the trade show booth, and finally declaring, "Omigod, Dan—you've created the new neutral!"

These plants do more than bridge the seasons, they expand them. Heucheras act in an almost evergreen fashion, retaining last season's leaves, and then go on to provide a very early flush of foliage (Dan remembers a midwinter Wisconsin garden where heucheras were the *only* color in the garden). Whether used stand-alone or en masse (Plate 116), *Heuchera* accepts whatever role we assign it and plays it with style. Heucheras are the perfect gardening friend!

Heucheras and bronze companion plants

Heucheras can either echo or contrast with bronze companion plants, depending on their *own* color—and sometimes they do both at once, as Pamela Harper (*Designing With Perennials*, 2001) explains: "[An echo is] some aspect of a plant repeated in another one nearby. . . . What pleases me so much about color echoes is, I think, that although united by similarities, there is also contrast." In this same classic title, Harper makes another excellent and, to our minds, original point when she says, "As harmonizers, I would rank the brownish colors gardeners know as 'purple' equally with soft white and the less light reflecting grays." We couldn't agree more. The popularity of the whole range of brown-leaved heucheras is testament to this. Heucheras like 'Chocolate Veil', 'Ebony and Ivory', and 'Smokey Rose' offer the garden designer a desirable copper through chocolate color foil; the warm qualities of these hybrid heucheras create a soothing and substantial contrast to the enthusiastic greens of spring and the bright notes of summer, and a sympathetic echo of the nostalgic chords of fall.

Heucheras of a like shade can nicely echo purple-to-bronze shrubs (*Berberis thunbergii* f. *atropurpurea* 'Atropurpurea Nana', *Corylus maxima* 'Purpurea', *Cotinus* 'Grace', *Physocarpus opulifolius* 'Diabolo', *Sambucus nigra* f. *porphyrophylla* 'Guincho Purple', *Viburnum opulus* 'Nanum', *V. sargentii* 'Onondaga', *Weigela florida* 'Foliis Purpureis') and are accentuated by bronze- to purpletoned plants, such as *Salvia officinalis* and cultivars of *Ajuga*, *Berberis*, *Carex*, and *Perilla*. Other herbaceous plants that do well as echoes of purple-leaved heuchs include *Actaea simplex* 'Black Negligee', *A. s.* 'Hillside Black Beauty', *Sedum album* subsp. *teretifolium* 'Murale', *S. telephium* 'Matrona', and *Viola* 'Mars'. In *Black Magic and Purple Passion* (2000), Karen Platt lists hundreds of such potential companion plants with bronzed or blackened leaves. With so many choices, we find it helpful to carry a few heuchera leaves to the nursery to mix, mingle, and match with the darkly colorful offerings.

Amber-colored hybrid heuchs like 'Marmalade' and 'Peach Flambé' are stunning contrasts to bronze companion plants. Nowhere in the world have we seen heucheras so well blended with native bronze-colored plants as in New Zealand: from the mats of the prickly *Acaena* to complementary bronze sedges to the towering spears of *Phormium* (New Zealand flax, especially darkleaved hybrids like 'Platt's Black'), heucheras play a bonding role on the horticultural stage Down Under.

The Germans and Dutch have provided endless hybrids of *Astilbe*, whose lacy, often bronzed leaves can be a nice counterpoint to coral bells; favorites include the compact 'Sprite' and 'Willie Buchanan'. China has given us *Artemisia lactiflora* Guizhou Group, a 3-foot-tall background plant with finely cut bronze foliage. Many selections of *Cotinus*, the smoke tree, have very dark foliage and fair height (some to 20 feet). Also from China are many *Persicaria* forms like 'Red Dragon', 'Compton's Form', and 'Brushstrokes', all of which can echo the hues of brown-leaved heucheras. Europe has given us dark polemoniums and geraniums like *Geranium pratense* Victor Reiter Junior strain (via California) to play with.

One of the best echoic companion plants for purple heucheras is *Clematis recta* 'Purpurea'; this herbaceous clematis is an awesome sight as it rises out of the earth in spring, its compound dark purplish brown leaves and stems covered in fine silver hairs. In one of Grahame's older display gardens, the aptly named 'Chocolate Ruffles' interacted beautifully as an underplanting to a lovely, random cluster of *Aquilegia vulgaris* 'William Guiness' with its bicolor flowers of white and smokey purple-black. In another location, the same hybrid heuch worked as the dominant planting with a colony of *Fritillaria michailovskyi* on one side and the deeply incised foliage of *Sambucus racemosa* 'Sutherland Gold' on the other.

Several herbs, like *Origanum* 'Hopley's Purple', purple basils (*Ocimum* cvs.), and dwarf nasturtiums (*Tropaeolum majus* cvs.), make good bronzy container companions for heucheras.

Heucheras and silver companion plants

Silver-colored plants conjure up images of the Mediterranean garden. These scintillating silver-grays, as Pamela Harper calls them, can be both a binding mortar to the mosaic of colorful flowering heucheras and an excellent contrast to other colors. Silver plants are also gaining more respect in our gardens. Why? They're usually more drought-resistant than their green-leaved counterparts and bring contrast, texture, and zing to a garden. One of the more appealing aspects of many of the hybrid heucheras is their own silvery veiling; varieties like 'Pewter Veil', 'Mint Frost', and 'Can Can' have a real boost to the designer's palette. Used with sensitivity, silvers and grays can make a garden look both lively and exotic without being too busy.

The amount of light in any given garden must be taken into account, of course; the high light levels of a garden in the arid West obviously cannot be compared to the lower sunlight of maritime gardens. Thus, a dazzling silver focus plant in Portland, Oregon, might be just another plant in Denver, one that blends in and harmonizes. The key here is the degree to which a plant reflects or absorbs light; it is this that determines whether a plant will be a symbol of serenity and softness or take on a brasher, "hey, look at me!" character. Take a silvery Colorado blue spruce: scattered about the property, they become a complete distraction in the garden; as a focus, however, it can be a good tree. In the same way, one should not incorporate herbaceous dazzlers unless one is prepared to go all the way and not hold back, in which case, strong whites may have to be employed, as will strong purples, blues, and softer yellows. In any case, the net effect should be pleasing—which is where the hybrid heuchera really comes into its own.

Do try some of the silver heucheras as a color echo to silver companion plants; the silver veiling that is such an exciting feature of many hybrid heucheras can be used to great effect with bulbs, azaleas, rhododendrons, and mountain laurels as well as de rigueur hostas, Siberian iris, and hellebores. Grahame has used them in a dry interior Canadian climate along with penstemons, agastaches, marrubiums, and such ornamental grasses as silvery blue *Agropyron pubescens* (ex Ray Brown, one of the bluest hardy grasses available), *Corynephorus canescens* (grey hair-grass), *Koeleria glauca*, and *Molinia caerulea* 'Variegata' (a great variegated bunch grass).

Purple-leaved heucheras like 'Purple Petticoats', 'Obsidian', and 'Velvet Night' contrast beautifully with silvered plants like *Stachys byzantina* and cultivars of *Dianthus* (especially the red-flowered forms), *Festuca*, *Lamium*, and *Sedum*. And don't miss the chance to set off the startling *Salvia przewalskii*, with its silver sheen over large, heart-shaped leaves that are pebbled like a new basketball. Centaureas have always had a following, and some of the funky, sculptural forms from Central Asia are finding their way into gardens; *Centaurea armata* is one such beast, with great spikes of silver not too unlike some of the exotic *Morina* species like *M. persica*. *Townsendia* is popular with the cognoscenti, especially in Colorado. Likely *Artemisia* species include the low-growing *A. glacialis* and *A. schmidtiana* 'Nana', and shrubbier types such as *A. ludoviciana* var. *latiloba* and *A. stelleriana* (not to mention the esteemed hybrid 'Powis Castle'). Some are scary spreaders, so do your homework before planting.

For containers, consider *Cerastium tomentosum* or the annual *Lotus berthelotii*. *Lamium* varieties like *L. maculatum* 'Beacon Silver' do well in larger containers, but they can be pushy.

Heucheras and yellow companion plants

The yellow flowers and gold foliage variants of many different plants and shrubs can be used to create superb complementary synergy with 'Chocolate Ruffles' and its bronze-leaved kin such as 'Cappuccino'. For shocking contrastful counterpoint, work purple-leaved heucheras against the gold foliage of *Hosta* 'August Moon', *H.* 'Little Aurora', *H.* 'Sun Power', and many others; *Origanum vulgare* 'Aureum'; or *Veronica* 'Buttercup'. Other yellow-to-golden herbaceous plants include *Carex buchananii* and its fellow New Zealand sedges; *Carex ciliatomarginata* 'Island Brocade', *C. c.* 'Island Fantasy'; *Filipendula ulmaria* 'Aurea'; *Fuchsia* 'Genii'; *Tricyrtis hirta* 'Golden Gleam', *T.* 'Gilty Pleasure'; and cultivars of *Hakonechloa macra*, *Lysimachia*, and *Narcissus*.

As an underplanting to woody plants, try heucheras as a contrast to yellow-to-golden shrubs (*Berberis thunbergii* 'Aurea', *Cornus alba* 'Aurea', *Hypericum* ×*inodorum* 'Summergold', *Ligustrum* 'Vicaryi', *Lonicera nitida* 'Baggesen's Gold', *Physocarpus opulifolius* 'Dart's Gold', *Spiraea japonica* 'Goldflame', *S. j.* 'Lisp'), or conifers (*Cedrus deodara* 'Golden Horizon', *Chamaecyparis obtusa* 'Fernspray Gold', *C. o.* 'Nana Aurea', *Chamaecyparis pisifera* 'Aurea', *C. p.* 'Strathmore', *Juniperus communis* 'Gold Cone', *Taxus baccata* 'Summergold').

Heucheras in the woodland garden

Woodlands can be lush, moss-draped oases of shade or they can be dry rock-strewn areas between trees in the Rocky Mountains. Fortunately heucheras are native to both extremes. Often heucheras are the first plants to go into the woodland borders or islands Grahame creates, as a designer and in his personal garden, in dry, inland British Columbia: here are the tough and beautiful species heuchs, resembling some of the more vigorous *Geranium* species like *G. macrorrhizum* and *G. dalmaticum*, with their stout rhizomes; there stand the hybrid heucheras, doughty sentinels, marking the new zones and encouraging experimentation in a woodland setting. Heucheras play a primary succession role (to use the ecological term): they make a new garden area attractive and inviting for other species to colonize and beautify. In a dry western North American garden, the silver heucheras really gleam; check out 'Silver Shadows' for a real blast.

For nearly twenty-five years, Dan has tended his moist Pacific Northwest woodland garden on a third-of-an-acre lot, where sixty-five different Japanese maples vie with coral bells for light, root space, and water. A good number of heucheras are sun lovers, so Dan has tried to find varieties that are more tolerant of deep shade. 'White Marble' and 'Green Spice' and its sister 'Mint Frost' have been workhorses, illuminating the edges of dark paths. 'Pewter Veil' and, surprisingly, the bronzy 'Cappuccino' and 'Chocolate Ruffles' have done well with only an hour of direct light a day, and 'Persian Carpet' has become a compelling if not awesome plant. Both the native *Heuchera micrantha* and *H. maxima* do well in dappled shade and provide much needed flowers. Plan for some individuals to get 3 to 4 feet wide in your designs, so that they remain integrated with the rest of the plantings. Plants of this dimension function well as demarcation points in your garden.

Xeriscaping with heucheras

Heucheras are perfect for xeriscapes (unwatered gardens in a dry climate), lending some much needed panache to an evolving sensibility. Because there is less water in a xeriscape, each plant needs more space; there isn't as much clutter of foliage, and, therefore, each heuchera becomes more of a feature, imparting a soulful focus to the wilder landscape. Stressed though they are by a dryer environment, the rhizome and good, strong stem base of heucheras readies them to produce an explosion of leaves and stylish flower stalks. Eventually each subtle flower withers and falls to the ground, creating a light, petal compost. Ah, the joys of a self-deadheading plant!

The hybrid heucheras, with their silveriness and texture, are a powerful ally in the gardener's campaign to beautify harsher, more exposed sites; and the purple hybrids particularly, endowed with richness and mystery, combine well with the silvers for dry but not sterile-looking gardens. Hybrids with pubescens genes display excellent tolerance of direct sunlight; 'White Marble', for example, shows no tendency toward leaf scorch, even in hot, dry summer climates, and so would be a good bet for a xeriscape.

The winter garden

The onset of cold weather does heucheras a real favor. Their color seems to jump right out at you; they look jazzy when other perennials look bedraggled and forlorn. Come fall, silvery veins net up on 'Pewter Veil', 'Cascade Dawn', and other dark-leaved plants; certain green-leaved heucheras ('Green Spice' and 'Mint Frost', for example) gain red and purple veins. Over the winter months, *Heuchera glabra*'s venation stands out against its red-purple winter color, and variegated sanguinea forms like *H. sanguinea* 'Splish Splash' are similarly adorned with electric-red venation. True, golden forms ('Lime Rickey', 'Amber Waves', 'Marmalade') do fade in the winter months, but that sets the stage for the intense freshness of their spring color.

More than anything, heucheras give us *something* to see in the depth of winter. In areas where hoarfrosts are common, heucheras make a wonderful canvas for Jack Frost. Various forms are more evergreen in different areas; experiment to find the best winter show, and keep all coral bells out of pounding winds to help them retain their color through the winter season.

Heucheras in floral design

Dan was sitting in the Chicago airport, travel-catatonic and bored to tears, when his cell phone sprang to life. It was his wife.

"Dan?"

"Uh, yeah . . ."

"Are you near a magazine stand?"

"Uh, yeah . . ."

"Go get the latest *Martha*—she's using your heuchera!"

Sure enough, on a spring-themed cover of velvet-black tulips in an oh-so-appropriate vase, Martha Stewart had used 'Chocolate Ruffles' leaves to echo and set off the voluptuous tulips. Another call came from a friend in the D.C. area, informing Dan that this was not the first time (nor would it be the last) those leaves had been singled out: the White House flower arranger had included them in small bouquets at a diplomatic banquet!

Heucheras have a lot to offer the florist and especially the homeowner, who can't always run out and buy some nice foliage and flowers. Their dainty flowers contrast well with the boldness of the foliage. With varieties like 'Veil of Passion', 'Cherries Jubilee' and 'Fireworks', the tonalities of the colored flowers and petioles perfectly integrate with the foliage color. Dan has always considered these plants "living bouquets" in the garden.

All hybrids, especially those with strong americana blood, have long vase life at room temperature, and the color palette for both flowers and foliage has grown vastly in the past ten years. Choices were once limited to flat green leaves and a shorter red flower stem; now there are flowers in various shades on cut stems to a yard tall and myriad combinations of exotic foliage in exciting shapes. Use your imagination to combine unorthodox materials like New Zealand sedge (*Carex buchananii*) and gold-toned foliage to contrast with the more purply leaves. Some heucheras ('Pewter Veil', for one) have long petioles that adapt beautifully to arrangements; mix some pewter tones into the rose and antique-whites of a Victorian centerpiece, or try 'Mardi Gras', with its festive splashing, in a birthday bouquet. 'Purple Petticoats' makes a lovely foil for the darkest roses.

In the late 1990s, Terra Nova Nurseries performed several generations of crosses with the 'Pruhoniciana' heucheras, which group of large-flowered hybrids resulted from generations of selections from tall-flowered *Heuchera cylindrica* and *H. sanguinea*, and whose interesting flower colors originally ranged from chartreuse to pink to browns and greeny reds. Terra Nova selected for superior color and backcrossed to their largest and brightest sanguineas to create the Wand series, designed for the florist trade and for flower arrangers (Plate 115); 'Magic Wand', 'Shamrock', and 'Florist's Choice', with their lovely wild look, work best in informal bouquets. Not only are their strong, stiff stems a florist's dream, the flower spikes last well and offer a flower shape uncommon in their trade. Other heucheras' flowers have good vase life but can shatter when bumped.

Leaves and flowers are best cut in the morning. Standard florist's rules apply, and preservative packets do help extend the flower life. Chrissie Harten, a floral instructor in Redditch, Worcestershire, England, is keen on using unusual materials, especially heucheras, in interesting ways. Here's a bit of the wealth of information you'll find at her Web site (http://www.thegardener .btinternet.co.uk/):

> For me, heucheras are the perfect plants for flower arranging. They are evergreen, so their foliage is available from my garden whenever I need it. They come in a wonderful variety of sizes, colors, and forms, from almost black, through to orange, green, and red coloring, some with frilly edges to their leaves, and some with plainer edges. There is always one kind which will suit my purpose whatever color scheme I am using. They give a wonderful contrast of color and form when used with other foliage and are superb to use in all-foliage arrangements. Most heucheras also have lovely flowers, which are a joy to use when in season. I particularly like using the flowers of *Heuchera sanguinea*, *H. cylindrica* 'Greenfinch', and *H.* 'Eden's Aurora'.
>
> Their foliage is very long-lasting; up to four weeks in water and slightly less in floral foam. As a teacher who demonstrates flower arranging every week, this means that I can reuse my heuchera foliage. I make sure that I leave plenty on my plants in the garden, where they will continue to look stunning all year round. The foliage "holds" well, without wilting, even if the floral foam is allowed to dry out somewhat. This is especially

useful when using heucheras in flower arranging competition work, when plant material must be capable of lasting well without any attention for the duration of the competition, which could be several days.

The darker-leaved heucheras look fabulous in arrangements when combined with yellow-leaved plants such as *Hedera helix* 'Buttercup', *Humulus lupulus* 'Aurea', *Philadelphus coronarius* 'Aureus', *Dicentra spectabilis* 'Gold Heart', *Geranium* 'Ann Folkard', or any of the yellow-leafed or yellow variegated hostas. The contrast in color makes heucheras leaves appear darker, and the yellow-leaved plants more yellow.

The generally rounded form of heuchera leaves combines well with taller, straighter plant material such as *Phormium*, *Iris*, *Crocosmia*, *Cordyline*, or *Equisetum hyemale*. In addition, they do well with more complex leaves such as *Mahonia*, *Grevillea*, and *Callistemon*, and grass-like foliage such as *Carex* and *Miscanthus*.

I often use foliage so that the underside is uppermost, as this is sometimes the more interesting side. Examples of this are *Rubus cockburnianus* 'Tricolor' and *Brachyglottis* 'Sunshine'. Heucheras also lend themselves to this treatment, as many of them have a beautiful pink flush to the underside of the leaves that gives them, quite literally, another dimension which looks stunning with other pink foliage and flowers.

Be creative and have fun with these new heuchs!

"Cooking" with heucheras

Here follow concoctions for gardens and containers, with heucheras as the chief ingredient. Thanks to Marietta O'Byrne, Mary Wilson, Cornell Farms, Proven Winners, and Ferguson's Fragrant Nursery for sharing their recipes.

Danielle's Monster Basket

Heuchera 'Purple Petticoats' (3)
Exclamation Point: *Pennisetum setaceum* 'Rubrum'
Trailers: *Ipomoea batatas* 'Blackie', I. b. 'Margarita'
Textural Counterpoints: *Marjoram* 'Golden', *Solenostemon (Coleus)* 'Merlot', S. 'Sedona', S. 'Dip't in Wine', S. 'Sky Fire'

Deb's Spring Surprise

Heuchera 'Can Can' (3)

Exclamation Point: *Phormium tenax* 'Bronze'

Textural Counterpoints: *Carex oshimensis* 'Evergold', *Euphorbia* 'Efanthia',
 Narcissus 'Quail', tulips (especially parrot tulips), *Viola* Sorbet series (or
 other light-colored violas)

Mary's Monster Container

Heuchera 'Black Beauty' (3)

Heuchera 'Vesuvius' (3)

Exclamation Point: *Phormium tenax* 'Bronze'

Trailer: *Geranium sessiliflorum* 'Red Select'

Textural Counterpoints: *Caryopteris* ×*clandonensis* 'Worcester Gold', *Corokia
 cotoneaster*, *Diascia* 'Hecbel' (Coral Belle), *Salvia coccinea* 'Brenthurst'

Fall Basket

Heuchera 'Amber Waves'

Exclamation Point: *Phormium* 'Platt's Black'

Textural Counterpoints: *Viola* 'Penny Orange', chrysanthemums for
 seasonal color

Mini-combos for the garden

* *Heuchera* 'Amber Waves', *Helleborus foetidus* 'Golden Showers',
 Ophiopogon spp.

* *Heuchera* 'Amber Waves', *Carex* 'Toffee Twist', *Nemesia* 'Intraigold'
 (Sunsatia Lemon), *Osteospermum* 'Seimora' (Orange Symphony)

* *Heuchera* 'Chocolate Ruffles', *Taxus baccata* Aurea Group

* *Heuchera* 'Chocolate Veil', *Geranium* 'Ann Folkard', *Lonicera nitida*
 'Baggesen's Gold'

* *Heuchera* 'Green Spice', *Carex comans* 'Frosted Curls'

* *Heuchera* 'Green Spice', *Eucomis comosa* 'Oakhurst', *Imperata cylindrica*,
 Tanacetum vulgare 'Isla Gold'

* *Heuchera* 'Marmalade', *Calibrachoa* 'Callie Sunset', *Nemesia* 'Inuppink'
 (Sunsatia Blackberry)

- *Heuchera* 'Obsidian', *Diascia* 'Hecbel' (Coral Belle), *Ophiopogon* spp.

- *Heuchera* 'Obsidian', *Diascia* 'Hecbel' (Coral Belle), *Impatiens* 'Mango'

- *Heuchera* 'Obsidian', *Calibrachoa* 'Sunbells Peach', *Lobelia erinus* 'Regatta Sky Blue'

- ×*Heucherella* 'Sunspot', *Berberis thunbergii* f. *atropurpurea* 'Atropurpurea Nana', *Primula* 'Wanda Cherry Red'

Sources

Hybrid seeds

B & T World Seeds
Route des Marchandes
Paguignan
34210 Aigues-Vives
France

Chiltern Seeds
Bortree Stile
Ulverston
Cumbria LA12 7PB
United Kingdom

Stokes Seeds Inc.
P.O. Box 548
Buffalo, NY 14240-0548

Thompson and Morgan
P.O. Box 1308
Jackson, NJ 08527-0308

Species seed

Alplains Seeds
Alan Bradshaw
P.O. Box 489
Kiowa, CO 80117-0489
Excellent collections over the years, including some high-elevation *Heuchera pulchella* and *H. sanguinea*.

Northwest Native Seeds
Ron Ratko
17595 Vierra Canyon Rd. #172
Prunedale, CA 93907
The former Seattle resident collects extensively throughout the West and offers many fine species from catalog to catalog.

Rocky Mountain Rare Plants
Rebecca Day-Skowron
1706 Deerpath Rd.
Franktown, CO 80116-9462
A good source, with mostly alpine species.

Sierra Seed Supply
358 Williams Valley Rd.
Greenville, CA 95947
California species from the inland areas.

Southwestern Native Seed
P.O. Box 50503
Tucson, AZ 85703
Sally and Tim Walker's seed company has been around a long time, and they occasionally offer species from Arizona, New Mexico, and Mexico.

Heucheras retail

Busse Gardens
17160 245th Ave.
Big Lake, MN 55309
tel: 763-263-3403
fax: 763-263-1473
e-mail:
customer.service@bussegardens.com
Web site: www.bussegardens.com
Mail order available, catalog $3.00.

Forest Farm
990 Tetherow Rd.
Williams, OR 97544
tel: 541-846-7269
fax: 541-846-6963
e-mail: plants@forestfarm.com
Web site: www.forestfarm.com
Mail order only, catalog $5.00.

Patrick Studios, Inc.
18 Haendel St.
Kirkland, QC H9H 4Y9
Canada
tel: 514-695-8399
fax: 514-695-7218
Web site: www.thegurugarden.com
Mail order in Canada only, catalog $5.00
Canadian.

Plant Delights Nursery, Inc.
9241 Sauls Rd.
Raleigh, NC 27603
tel: 919-772-4794
fax: 919-662-0370
e-mail: office@plantdel.com
Web site: www.plantdelights.com
Mail order available; send ten stamps
or a box of chocolates for a catalog, if
you like.

The Primrose Path
921 Scottdale-Dawson Rd.
Scottdale, PA 15683
tel: 724-887-6756
fax: 724-887-3077
e-mail: primrose@a1usa.net

Wayside Gardens
1 Garden Lane
Hodges, SC 29695
toll-free: 800-213-0379
e-mail: info@waysidecs.com
Web site: www.waysidegardens.com

Heucheras wholesale

Epic Plant Company
RR 2, East and West Line
Niagara-on-the-Lake, ON L0S 1J0
Canada
e-mail: inquire@epicplants.com

JEA Perennials
Strathroy, ON N7G 3H5
Canada
tel: 519-245-4039
toll-free: 877-500-6162
Web site: www.jeaperennials.com

Mori Nurseries Ltd.
RR 2
Niagara-on-the-Lake, ON L0S 1J0
Canada
tel: 905-468-3217
fax: 905-468-7271
e-mail: mori@morinurseries.com

Terra Nova Nurseries, Inc.
P.O. Box 23938
Tigard, OR 97281-3938
toll-free: 800-215-9450, ext. 305
fax: 503-263-3152
e-mail: sales@terranovanurseries.com
Web site: www.terranovanurseries.com

Valleybrook Gardens, Ltd.
1831 Peardonville Rd.
Abbotsford, BC V4X 2M3
Canada
tel: 604-855-1177
fax: 604-855-1177

Index of Heucheras and Heucherellas